3

len

5136

Planning for profit

Also by
Ian Holden and Peter K. McIlroy

NETWORK PLANNING
IN MANAGEMENT CONTROL SYSTEMS

IAN HOLDEN AND PETER K. McILROY

PLANNING
FOR
PROFIT

HUTCHINSON OF LONDON

HUTCHINSON CO (PUBLISHERS) LTD
3 Fitzroy Square, London, W.1.

London Melbourne Sydney Auckland
Wellington Johannesburg Cape Town
and agencies throughout the world

First published 1973

Printed in Great Britain by Redwood Press Limited, Trowbridge, Wiltshire
and bound by Wm. Brendon, of Tiptree, Essex.

ISBN 0 09 113980 5

Contents

Part Two—Case Studies

3 *Simple manual methods*

4 *More advanced method—an example based on a large planning study*

5 *Examples of use in the construction industry*

Part Three—Further Developments

6 *Towards the development of a fully integrated data
processing system for operational and financial control*

7 *A philosophy of management*

Illustrations

Acknowledgements

We are grateful to a number of individuals and organisations for permission to reproduce material or to base our examples on work done under their control. These include the following:

Freeman Fox and Associates and Mr. J. O. Tresidder, Managing Director, for permission to use examples of work done on the Land Use/Transportation Study for East Central Scotland (Chapter 4) and the Grangemouth/Falkirk Growth Area Road Study (Chapter 3).

Rendel, Palmer and Tritton, Consulting Engineers, for permission to draw on experience related to their design of the turbine house frame at Aberthaw 'A' Power Station. (Chapter 5)

John Morgan (Builders) Limited who were the civil engineering contractors for the Power Station, and Mr. S. A. Vincent who was Chief Engineer/Agent for the firm.

International Computers Ltd., (ICL) for permission to reproduce extracts from their PERT Manuals.

Computation, Research and Development Ltd., (CRD) for agreeing to references to various computer programs.

A'Court Photographs Limited for photograph (Fig 5.9) of Aberthaw Power Station.

Preface

This is a highly competitive age. If you want to make a profit you have to plan your work carefully; you have to be able to estimate how much things are going to cost; you need to know, at frequent intervals throughout your project, whether your estimates are working out right in practice and whether you are, in fact, likely to make a profit. In other words, you need a tailor-made management control system linked closely to your Project Plan.

In our previous book *Network Planning in Management Control Systems* we set out our views on how to establish such conditions. Reactions to that book have shown us that there is a need to expand our ideas and show how they can be applied in practice. This is the purpose of this present book.

In our first two chapters we deal with the underlying theory and basic methods which, we maintain, can be applied with suitable modification to almost any task in which the need is for careful planning and controlled execution in order to achieve the necessary profit margin.

The following three chapters show how these theories and methods can be applied in three widely different types of project. Chapters 3 and 4 are based on actual examples of the use of the method while in Chapter 5 we show how, with the advantage of hind-sight, we think we would have applied the method to a complex problem in the field of civil engineering construction. As these chapters have been reproduced as self-contained case studies there is some repetition which we hope the reader will accept as contributing to the completeness of each.

We recognise that there is still scope for improvement and innovation in integrated control systems, particularly with the increased use of the computer, and in Chapter 6 we suggest how a fully integrated system could be designed for use in planning and controlling a number of projects simultaneously to provide a really effective and efficient management tool.

In the final chapter we survey our own management experience over the past ten years. From this we try to draw some conclusions on the balance between flair and system in modern management and attempt to set down our philosophy for it in the 1970's.

Part one - Theory

1 The principles of integrated control

1.01 The profitable employment of resources

Management's concern with the profitable employment of resources has led increasingly to the adoption of sophisticated techniques to measure the significance of past events and to predict the future as accurately as possible. This book is concerned particularly with improving the efficiency of project management through the creation of a coherent, planned system which:

1 Enables current performance to be assessed
2 Enables critical decisions to be made about immediate future operations
3 Enables the overall profitability of the project to be reviewed and controlled.

After explaining the basic concepts of costing and planning on which an integrated operational and financial control system relies, we develop our approach to this subject through examples of projects of differing type and complexity, illustrating ways in which both manual and computer systems can be used.

Our previous book *Network Planning in Management Control Systems, Hutchinson Educational 1970,* sets out the basis of our general approach, and readers may find it useful to refer to that book. Fig. 1.1, which is derived from this earlier book, illustrates the main tasks involved in setting up an integrated control system for a project. This diagrammatic representation sets out the basic steps in the planning process in relation to the

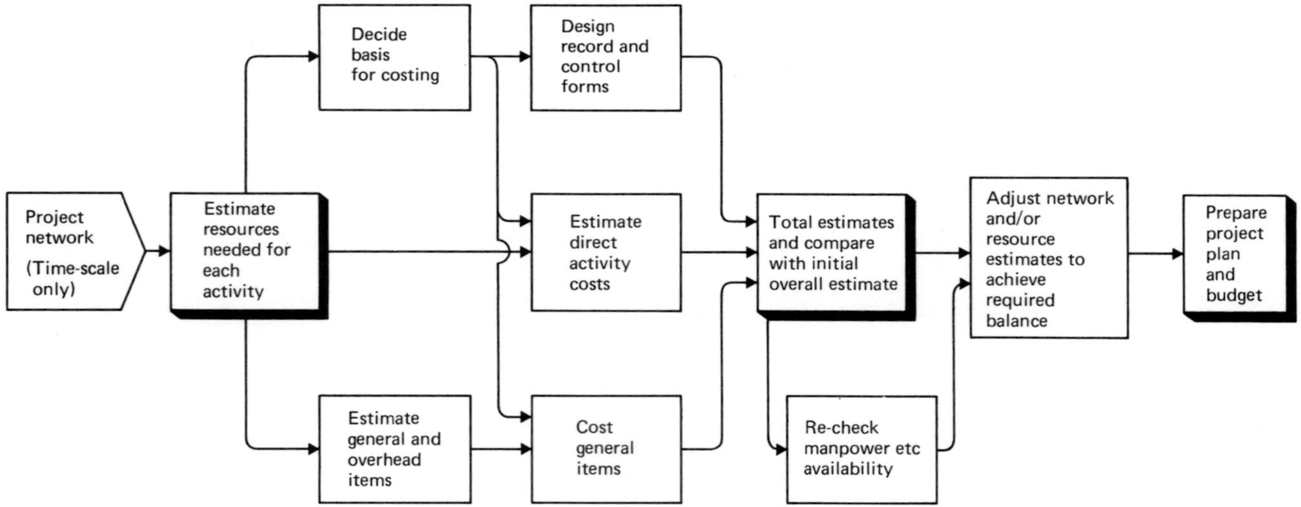

Fig. 1.1 Main steps in creating integrated control

management purpose, and illustrates the importance of planning the basis of the control system itself before applying network techniques to a project.

It is also important to understand the link between the desired management purpose and the related complexity of the necessary planning and control system. (See Fig. 1.2.)

As our present book is concerned with a specific management purpose, *to plan and control profit*, it will be seen that a complete control system is required. This purpose implies, in terms of management technique, that it will be necessary to integrate many elements of business operations and to develop systems and methods of working of an advanced and possibly sophisticated nature.

The size of a project is no bar to this general approach to planning. It merely affects the methods of communication and data processing and alters the scale of management and organisation. The project manager still has to apply the same principles, and if he is to achieve this particular purpose it is essential that he understands fully the steps which are involved. Having rationalised this he should set about building his project control system methodically, leading at least to step 12 in the planning scale, as illustrated in Fig. 1.2.

These twelve steps which the project manager will have to take can be summarised as follows:

1: Making an appreciation of the project, defining carefully the overall aim, the basic objectives and the main component parts.

2: Providing a preliminary descriptive network diagram—known as the *landscape*.

3: Setting the scale for control of the project.

4: Producing from these first three basic elements a *project plan*. (This becomes the foundation of analysis upon which the project manager can build the next steps.)

5: Carrying out operational planning involving the production of basic bar chart schedules for the project and the main organisational elements concerned—persons, sections, departments or organisations.

6, 7: Carrying out phasing and/or resource planning to adjust or 8: the project plan to the realities of resource availability.

9: Establishing the basis for resource costing. This is a key step as can be seen by reference to Figs. 1.1 and 1.2

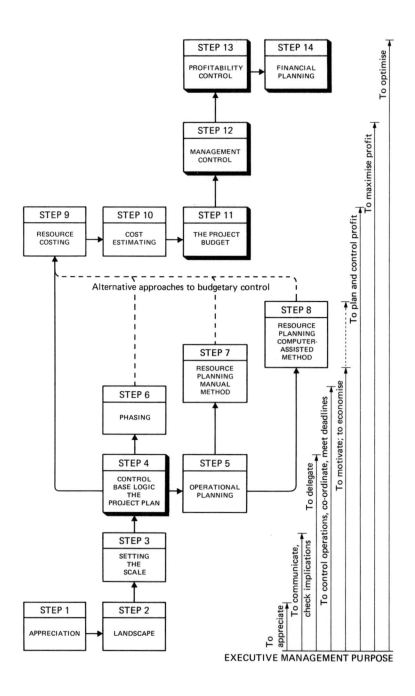

Fig. 1.2   Relationship between steps in the planning process

involving accounting, administration and data processing services within the organisation as a whole.

(It should be remembered at this stage that the project manager intent upon planning and controlling profit will not have to carry out all the above stages in strict sequence; only one of steps 6, 7 and 8 is required depending on the complexity of the project and the data. He must, however, move through all the other steps within this overall process. It is essential that he establishes and agrees the requisite working arrangements at this stage with the administration of his own organisation; this has far-reaching implications for the organisation whose administrative processes must be adapted to suit project control if the remaining steps are to have a substantial base to build on. This point is dealt with in greater detail in Chapter Two.)

10: Carrying out cost estimating in relation to the project plan, its phasing and operational aspects, and the basic resource estimates.
11: Establishing on this basis a project budget which will be so constructed and linked to the administrative and accounting processes as to give the required sensitivity of control.
12: Planning the provision for adequate management control, which involves the method of collection, collation and analysis of current cost data and the production of well-founded management reports on the status of the project.

At this early stage of the book we have felt it necessary to spell out this step-by-step basis for a management control system to remind readers that their approach to *Planning for Profit* in their own projects must be:

thorough
systematic
economical
carefully planned

Very often organisational environments may be alien to this approach and thus frustrate it. The project manager may therefore find himself 'on his own'. It is obviously easier if the organisation adopts an overall approach and sets up a suitable management accounting and data processing system. It may, however, be difficult in some situations to provide such an administrative basis for all the projects handled by the organisation, although senior management should think very carefully at policy level before deciding against a centralised control system. The alternative can only be that each major project has its own individual management and control process, which may be significantly less efficient. In such a case the project manager has to take responsibility for estimating, accounting and administrative processes, in addition to all his other responsibilities, possibly upsetting the optimum balance which should be struck between his technical control of the project and his operational and financial control.

While the advantages of a well understood system on the basis described are enormous, we recognise that the decision on whether to operate it at company level or at project level must be made by each individual company and that the system itself must be kept within sensible limits of cost and management time usage.

1.02 Towards an integrated system

We have outlined the twelve basic steps needed to create a management control system which enables the project manager to plan and control his profit. The remainder of this book is concerned with how to go about doing this in procedural terms, and with case studies which are based on project management where these ideas have been tried and tested. Three basic ideas need to be spelt out before proceeding further. This form of planning is concerned with:

1 The future, and thus with cost forecasting, estimating and planning
2 Current performance, and thus with the recording, collation and analysis of actual costs
3 Forming a link between 1 and 2 for purposes of comparison
4 Activities within the project plan* as cost centres.

The effect of basing both forecasting and the recording of actual performance on activities is two-fold:

---

* Project Plan: the basic control framework

PROJECT NO. | **POSITION AT END OF MARCH 1971**

(Name of Project)		TOTAL TO END DEC. 70	JAN	FEB	MAR	APRIL	MAY	JUNE	JULY	AUG	TOTAL BUDGET	AMOUNT SPENT	% SP.	% COMP.	VALUE OF WORK DONE	REMARKS
011 General Preliminaries	B	650	–	–	–						650			100	650	—
	A	520	110	–	–							630	97			
012 Prepare zone Plan	B	50	150	–	–						200			100	200	Began late; completed about 1 month late.
	A	–	78	152	10							230	115			
013 Prepare street index	B	–	2.50	200	–						460			100	450	Late be... ...target.
	A	–	110	380	30							510	114			
014 Obtain census data	B	100	100	100	100	100								50	250	Somewhere over the target rate of expenditure: action needed
	A	72	125	60	157	100										
021 Design survey	B	50		260	–						650			100	650	Completed on time.
HOME INTERVIEW SURVEY	A											335	51			
033 Conduct roadside survey	B	–	–	100	790	930					1,820			35	640	Slightly behind schedule due to bad weather.
	A	–	–	63	632							695	38			
070 Code roadside survey	B	–	–	–	350	850	700				1900			20	380	Well up on target so far.
	A	–	–	–	290							290	15			
									TOTALS		7,250	5,622			5,280	Reasonably in balance.

Fig. 1.3 Typical monthly summary report for management

1 Traditional accounting or budgeting systems must be modified as they are seldom helpful to project management mainly because costs are not usually coded or allocated to activities but to accounting cost groups. These are usually designed for ease of collection, verification and analysis of costs which are then used in the production of financial accounts, culminating in a yearly profit and loss account and balance sheet, as required by the Companies' Acts. Furthermore, most cost accounting systems in commercial, industrial or manufacturing organisations are based on standard or marginal costs which are not collected or analysed by activity

2 When the project manager creates even a simple manual system of cost forecasting and analysis by activity, he can immediately achieve a much better management control over the profitability of his project.

The core of our system of integrated operational and financial control for projects is therefore contained in the concepts of "activity costing" and "value of work done" as it enables a link to be established between these two elements. Even when this link is created in a project plan there are still practical administrative problems to be resolved, and rules have to be established for activity cost accounting to enable the project manager to review his progress periodically. In Fig. 1.3 a monthly project report is reproduced which brings together such data in the form of forecast and actual costs. It also illustrates the measurement of value of work done.

In the following chapters these points will be explored in greater detail. We examine and illustrate their application to projects of differing complexities, from a manual analysis for a small project, through a partially computerised system applying separate programs for network analysis and cost accounting. Finally we outline some ideas for an integrated data processing system for operational and financial control.

What then are the basic steps which the project manager must take to forge the link between operational and financial planning?

These are set out in Fig. 1.4 and will be described in greater detail in Chapter Two. They rest on the foundation of a control base network or "project plan" and whilst we assume that the reader will understand the significance of these terms it is

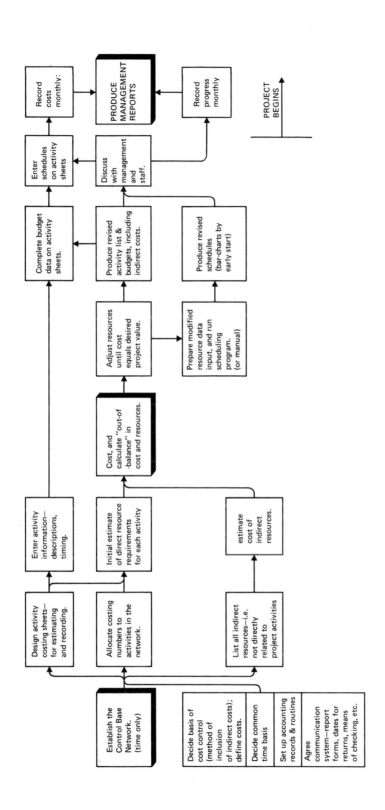

Fig. 1.4 Setting up an integrated control system

perhaps worthwhile spelling this out in a little more detail.

Establishing the control base network (project plan) is in our opinion a critical step in setting up an integrated system and is needed by the project manager whether he is starting from scratch or whether he has had previous experience of setting up a control system. The network in Fig. 1.4 assumes that he has not developed such a system previously and it has two main elements:

1 setting up the costing system
2 carrying out the process of activity costing.

These, however, spring from the project plan and must be developed in the knowledge that it will be used as the basis for activity costing and for budgetary control. In order to evolve a rational, economic system it will have been constructed with particular attention to the scale of cost of the separate parts of

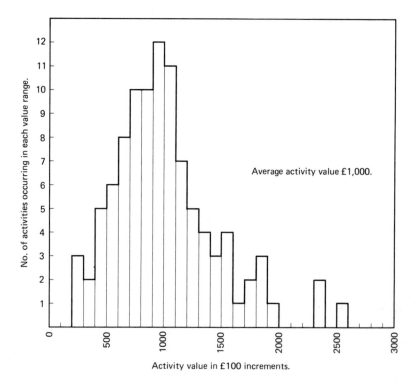

Fig. 1.5   Typical distribution of activity values for budgetary control

the network. For example, a contract of value £100,000 could be analysed into 100, 500 or 1,000 or more activities.

Even if it is sensible for technical reasons to go into a relatively large number of activities, it is generally not sensible to do so from a budgetary control point of view. The control base for the project from which the phased project plan is developed should be decided after estimating the size and value of activities which will give a sufficiently sensitive review mechanism for the purpose of budgetary control. In a particular case a 100 activity network might thereby lead to an average activity value of, say, £1,000. The range of activity values might be in this case between £100 and £10,000, as shown in Fig. 1.5.

For budgetary control purposes a decision about the average value is important, as a relatively simple framework for the allocation and analysis of costs is desirable. This stems from the practical necessity to keep the work of regular monthly data processing within reasonable bounds and at the same time to give the project manager an uncluttered view of overall progress.

1.03 Towards effective management control

The project manager must therefore approach the decision on the number of activities in his control base network with the practical problems of monthly management control in mind, as well as the technical control of the project. Technical control can be improved where necessary by more detailed sub-networking and a further breakdown of activities; these can be kept out of the main stream of the project plan network and its attendant costing processes.

Thus by one means or another the project manager can decide upon a convenient average activity value. In addition, he should take into account at this stage the average duration of an activity, knowing that a monthly cost analysis is to be carried out during progress of the project. If, for example, the project is to take one year to complete there will be a considerable amount of over-lapping between activities and on average the manager will be examining the progress of perhaps eight to ten main costed activities each month. The decision about the level of detail required for management control is bound up very closely with overall duration and thus with average activity duration.

Before finalising the decision on the number of activities a further point should be considered. It may be that compatibility between different projects of a similar type within the organisation is a desirable feature of a cost control system; this can be important when comparing costs for one particular type of activity from several different jobs when making an estimate for a new job. There may be a case, therefore, for having either more or fewer activities in the network than would at first appear to be the appropriate number.

The treatment in this book is based upon a monthly cycle review. We recognise that in some cases it is necessary to have weekly, daily or even hourly reviews; the same cost control considerations will apply for project management.

A simple guide to the decision on the number of activities is shown in Fig. 1.6.

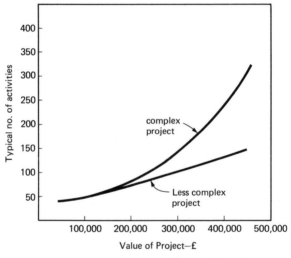

Fig. 1.6   Example of typical relationship between number of activities and project value

It should be emphasised that this is merely an illustration of our own experience of certain types of project and may not apply to some other types. Notwithstanding this, it can be seen from the diagram that the emphasis is on keeping down the number of activities to a level which can be used efficiently in the data processing and management information system. However, a further variation may be introduced at this stage. If it is thought that a project of value of £200,000 requires some 150 activities in the project control network for a project period of say, eighteen months, it may be necessary to increase the number of activities considerably if the project period has to be reduced to say, twelve months, reflecting the greater intensity of control which is needed in such a case. This indicates that there may be a time-cost relationship such as that illustrated in Fig. 1.7.

This is purely hypothetical. It is likely that increased value will require a more detailed project plan network while increased duration may or may not require more detail. The decision on detail must be made in the knowledge of the organisation concerned, the grouping and delegation of responsibility within the organisation and the practical arrangements for the necessary administrative procedure.

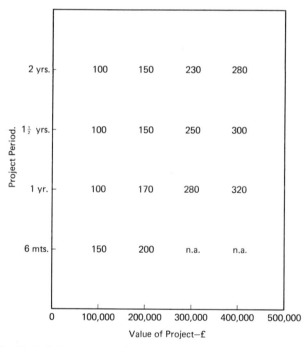

Fig. 1.7   Typical time—cost relationship in projects and the initial number of activities required for cost control

1.04 Criteria for constructing the project plan

The main criteria for the project manager to consider in constructing his project plan (i.e. control base network) will therefore be those of:

1 technical control requirements
2 requirements of the organisation.

The reader may think that this point has been over-emphasised, but in our opinion it is vital that at this basic stage of developing a control system the project manager should understand and make his decision objectively, with the clear intention of obtaining effective control of the profitability of the project. Too often the project control is developed at arm's-length from the project manager. It is little wonder that—lacking the information or insight about the real economies and priorities of a project—a remote project planning service can produce an unwieldy, insensitive or administratively complicated system. *Too often the emphasis has been on a very detailed logic and resource analysis without integrating the system with cost planning and control.* The resulting profits have thus not matched up to what could be legitimately expected from the introduction of the "new technique".

2 - The formulation of integrated control, administrative procedures and resource costing

2.01 Introduction

Fig. 1.4, which illustrated the formulation of an integrated control system, showed that at the outset there are four separate procedures to be carried out. These are:

1 The design of activity costing sheets
2 The allocation of cost numbers to activities
3 The construction of a comparative basis for costing
4 The establishment of related accounting procedures.

These form the basis of "resource costing" providing the means for the calculation, recording and analysis of forecast costs, together with their direct comparison with actual costs recorded during the progress of the project, in an established data processing framework.

2.02 The activity cost form

In our integrated planning and costing system each activity becomes a cost centre for planning, estimating and reviewing the progress of work. A form devised by the authors for their own work is shown in Fig. 2.1.

As a separate cost centre it incorporates a simple means by which all the basic aspects of the activity are described and recorded both before and during the project, and provides for:

(i) *A description and cost coding of the activity*—The description of an activity in this context can be extremely important, and much of the value of an

15

integrated system can be lost if these are not clear and easily understood. The project manager should try to avoid the possibility of error in the allocation of time (= cost) by members of staff during the course of the project, by making sure that every activity is clearly and precisely defined from the outset

(ii) *A record of the start, progress and completion of the activity, both planned and executed*—This gives a visual check on progress against plan. The concepts of float and critical activities can be applied to bring out wider and often hidden implications of delay or cost over-run

(iii) *Planned resource data including descriptions and costs*—This amounts to a check list of the effort which is to be put into each activity and is built up during resource/cost planning and summarised here when finalised.

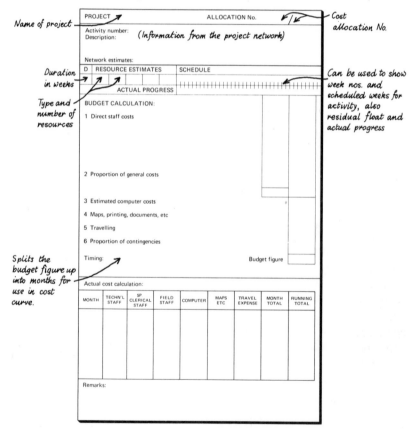

Fig. 2.1   Typical activity cost form

Where management and manpower are both costed this has the further implication of setting down the key personnel involved and their hourly rate, with a direct bearing on the proposed method of delegation and responsibility. Depending on the nature of the project, the sheet may also provide a breakdown of the planned costs in different categories of cost, such as direct and indirect staff costs and various expenses

(iv) *Actual cost data related to relevant resources each month and giving a running total*—This section is necessary in principle, but may be modified to an extent, depending upon the scope of the computer program, if any, used for costing. Much more detailed descriptions of operating systems will be given in later Chapters, but the importance of this section of the form should not be ignored as it will provide a reliable basis for the analysis of performance. It will also provide invaluable information to the organisation for estimating similar work in the future

(v) *Remarks* to be recorded by the project manager, with the idea of explaining any special feature of the calculation of planned or actual cost recorded on the sheet.

It should be noted at this stage that the concept of an activity cost form does not become modified where a fully computerised system is introduced; it simply becomes part of the basic monthly print-out for the project. Whether in a manual or computerised system it remains the key to successful control.

The activity cost form is therefore a central component of the system providing for the recording of planned and actual cost. Its importance lies, however, in the assumption, not so far spelled out, that these are directly comparable. To ensure an acceptable degree of comparability involves certain technical problems, not the least of which is the time basis upon which costs are recorded, verified and paid. Network planning in fact helps to resolve this problem in part, but an understanding and sympathetic working relationship between the project manager and the administration of the company is still required.

In aggregate the activity cost forms provide the input to the management control reports used in budgetary planning and control. It should be noted that, as a matter of procedure, in the initial estimating stage these forms are only completed after the cost planning procedures have been carried out—see Fig. 1.4. Other forms to be described later are also used during the cost planning and budget balancing phase.

2.03 The allocation of cost numbers

The numbering system for projects and activities should be kept as simple as possible. A number is designated to represent each individual activity so that costs can be allocated, collated and identified by this number for data processing.

However, if the numbers are allocated systematically they can also be used in the data processing as the means for aggregation of activities into sub-groups or into total project costs, and for all activities into company totals. It becomes possible with such a system to carry out comprehensive analyses of cost. For example, a summary statement can be produced which shows all the costs incurred by the organisation for all projects on productive work by staff, backed up by a summary of non-productive costs (i.e. general indirect costs). Later in the book case studies and illustrations will reinforce this point and demonstrate the features of a computerised costing system.

At this stage it is sufficient to give a simple description of a numbering system which has been found to be effective for activity costing. Each new project is allocated an unique three-digit number which becomes its overall identity reference, for example 760. The activities in the control base network are then allocated subsidiary numbers within this group, for example 760/360. Thus a six-digit code is built up. Three-digit numbers have been found sufficient for projects within our experience but there may be cases where four-digit numbers are required. A typical system of cost allocation numbers is illustrated in Fig. 2.2.

Where projects running within the organisation are of a broadly similar nature there are obvious advantages in obtaining a relatively constant grouping of project costs, as this automatically aids identification by the staff and management, all of whom must be sufficiently familiar with the coding structure to allocate costs through weekly or monthly time sheets. The grouping system of cost allocation numbers also acts as a check on the completeness of the project plan.

Project No.		Activity No.	Description.
			Preliminaries
760	/	011	General preliminaries
760	/	012	Prepare zone plan
760	/	013	Prepare street index
760	/	014	Obtain and record census data.
			Home Interview Survey
760	/	021	Design survey
760	/	022	Select sample
760	/	023	Select and train staff
760	/	024	Conduct survey
760	/	025	Coding
760	/	026	Edit and tabulate program
760	/	027	Edit and tabulate.
			Roadside Survey
760	/	031	Design survey
			-etc.-
			Indirect Costs (not allocated to specific activities)
760	/	900	General Direction
760	/	901	Direction of data analysis staff.
760	/	902	Direction of drawing office staff.
			-etc.-

Fig. 2.2   Typical list of activity numbers, grouped for easy aggregation and
processing

We have placed particular emphasis on the need, both in the
design of the activity cost form and in the allocation of activity
cost numbers, to tie in with administrative and accounting
routines. We intend to show the importance of relating the
project planning system to the company's procedures as a
whole, as the steps needed to ensure that a comparative basis is
obtained have a strong bearing on the method of collection,
verification, allocation and analysis of actual costs and their
time base must also be considered.

2.04 Constructing a comparative basis for planned and actual costs

We will assume that a plan has been produced at the time when
a project starts, which forecasts a spend curve as shown in
Fig. 2.3.

This can be computed from the final adjusted activity start
dates and the scheduled activity resources and costs. Such a
curve is automatically produced in certain computer software

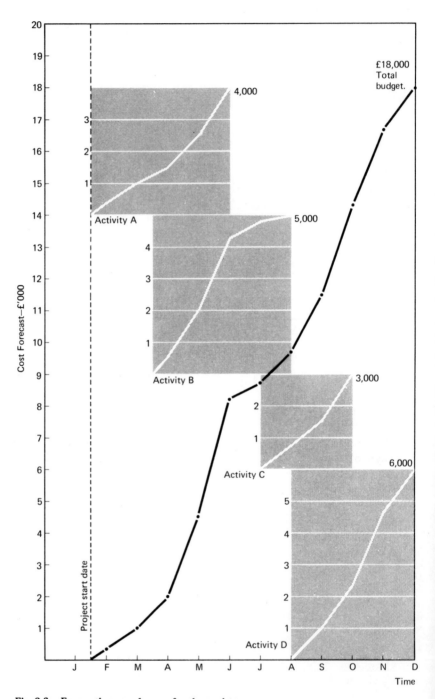

Fig. 2.3 Forecasting spend curve for the project

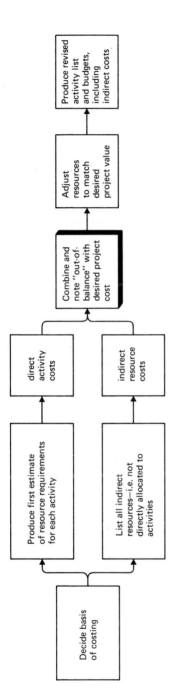

Fig. 2.4 Producing a balanced budget for the project

(for example ICL PERT).

A costed project plan with a spend curve of this type is produced through the adjustment of activities to acceptable starting dates within the available float and related to the requisite resources and their costs and availability. It will be obvious at once to the informed reader that a variety of spend curves could result from a network in different stages of refinement. This is accepted, and the real problem is to create a

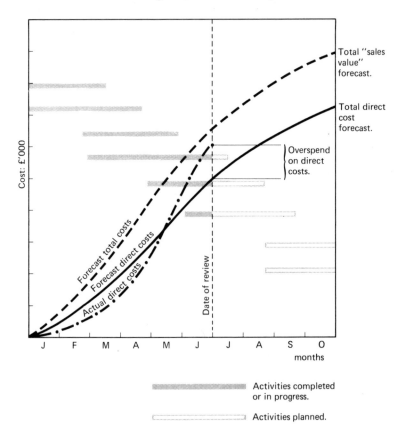

Fig. 2.5　Forecast and actual costs—measurement of progress (direct cost)

balanced forecast of activities, together with the resources required, within acceptable limits of time and cost. Fig. 2.4, which is derived from part of Fig. 1.4, shows what has to be done at this stage.

Before carrying on to describe the activity estimating and balancing sequence, it is necessary to decide the basis of cost control. The choice lies between, on the one hand, the use of basic costs and, on the other, the use of the sale value of the activity.

Each may have particular advantages in different circumstances. (a) In the first case the basis is that all costs of labour, materials, services and equipment are accounted for "at cost" whilst forecasting future spending. They are also recorded at actual cost when they are incurred. In terms of measurement this means that a separate computation is necessary to establish the relationship between incurred costs, budgets (activity based) and the project contract sum. Profit at any one stage will therefore have to be estimated on the basis of an over-run or under-run on forecast amounts, and will depend on the valuation of work in progress, with an estimated value given to work partly done. This is a common accounting practice. Where the convention leads to valuing work at cost for a project in progress it is difficult for the project manager to measure his overall progress effectively.

A simple measure of progress might be computed by projecting the actual cost curve (see Fig. 2.5). However, this could be highly misleading as the project obviously started much more slowly than planned and has required a rapid build up of costs subsequently to achieve acceptable progress—a not untypical situation. The value of work done to date is difficult to ascertain in these circumstances, not least because of the accounting problems relating to the time-base on which costs are recorded and reported in relation to planned costs through time. Assuming that no time-cost comparison problem exists, then the value of work carried out is probably best estimated by:

1 Adding back an "adjusted" profit element to each completed activity (adjusted to calculate a new profit percentage rate)

2 Assessing the activities in progress by estimating costs required to complete them, calculating activity cost

over-runs, deducting over-runs not recoverable through claims from planned profit, and valuing work in progress at cost plus an adjusted profit rate

3 Adjusting the forecasts for future activities (not yet started) to take account of new information.

The importance of these steps and the difficulty in applying them to estimate the value of work done can be illustrated by the recent case histories of several large British companies. A profit forecast in such circumstances is so difficult to calculate that it may be better for the project manager to limit comparison to actual costs to date against planned cost to date (time based allowed for). It is, however, vital for the project manager to have information which is as accurate as possible because he has to decide in these circumstances what action to take in order to adjust his spending to planned rates in relation to progress, or if necessary to establish claims or additional budget sums.

(b) In the second case, all activities are "costed" on the basis of the sale value of the item. The basic reason supporting this approach is that income is obtained by "selling" services at a price designed to cover overheads and profit. In the case of professional consultants, for example, charges are made for the time spent by professional staff at an hourly rate which is directly related to their salaries (i.e. to direct costs) with all other out-of-pocket expenses charged at cost. In such cases the basic hourly rate charged for each member of staff covers his salary and the cost of housing him in an office and providing all the necessary ancillary services, for example administration, machines, etc., together with the necessary profit margin. As activity costs are built up in terms of professional staff rates, together with the basic costs for services, equipment and materials, the activity cost forecast relates to the sale value of the activity and the sum of all the individual activity costs is equal to the total project budget.

With this method (measurement in terms of sale value) at any period of review, the value of work done can be measured by multiplying the activity value by the percentage of that activity completed. This can be compared with the percentage of that activity budget spent to that date, the difference directly reflecting the full effect on the project of any over-run or under-run. This comparison is illustrated in Fig. 2.6.

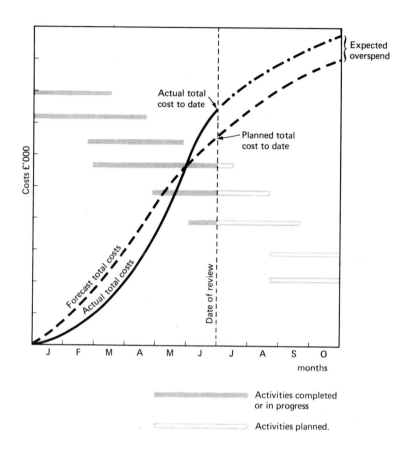

Costs £'000

Expected overspend

Actual total cost to date

Planned total cost to date

Forecast total costs

Actual total costs

Date of review

J F M A M J J A S O

months

Activities completed or in progress

Activities planned.

Notes: 1. Cost curves overlaid on activity bar chart.
       2. The advantage of determining progress by applying the sales value of all costs is that it is simpler to predict "overspend" at the end of the project, which is more meaningful than overspend at time "now".

Fig. 2.6   Forecast and actual costs—measurement of progress (sale value)

The full economic value of an over-run is therefore forecast and an element of lost profit opportunity is taken into account, thus reflecting on company performance overall. The method of applying this approach is described in a later section. It will be seen that the calculation of activity costs is in fact built up from actual costs initially and the overhead element is interpreted in relation to the activity and to the project as a whole.

2.05 Preliminary estimates of activity costs

We have now described three basic elements which are necessary to establish an activity based cost control system

1 The activity cost form
2 The activity coding system
3 The means of measurement and comparison between planned and actual costs.

Alongside these are other necessary administrative measures concerned with the collection, analysis and allocation of actual costs which will be described later. At this stage we are still concerned with forecasts—having ensured that they are based on the same principles for coding, measurement, recording and timing, which will apply to actual costs.

The project manager now has to look in much greater detail than previously at his *project plan*—that is, his control base network. He must make an initial allocation of budget sums available to these activities, taking into account the fundamental management thinking about the project. These allocations will be built up from information used at the initial estimating (or negotiating) stage of the project. Often that stage has been based on a different procedure, related more to company experience than to detailed networking, in which case the project manager has the problem of converting one set of estimates into an allocation across activities.

It is desirable that in the initial estimate a simplified form of network should be used to build up the offer, and wherever possible the project manager should be involved. Whatever approach is adopted, the realities of carrying out the project after winning the contract must lead to a more detailed analysis of the resources and techniques to be applied. This involves the building up of a project plan as a descriptive logic in which the basic components and stages of the work are set out. It may or may not be considered appropriate to carry out resource-cost calculations at this early stage, and in fact it is usual to approach network planning in two main parts:

1 Time Analysis
2 Resource Analysis

In most circumstances this is better than trying to combine both sets of calculations, as uncertainties over timing in relation to resources and costs can lead to expensive computer runs. This is true even where relatively advanced computer software is used. An agreed time-based network is therefore produced as a basis for the further calculations. Subjective judgements about resources are inevitable in doing this, but detailed work on resources is best left until later.

The time-based network is the starting point for detailed resource and cost forecasts. These forecasts divide into two basic elements—direct activity costs and indirect costs not specifically allocated to activities but directly relevant to the project.

The activity costing form has already been described (Fig. 2.1). It is used to record information about the activities such as description, duration and timing. Information concerning float and the global budget value is also completed. Detailed forecasts of labour, materials, equipment and other resources are now listed and basic costing rates are applied to all items within the activity.

Fig. 2.7 shows a useful form for recording the results of this first calculation for each activity.

In certain computer software there are facilities for doing these calculations, but in many cases an unsatisfactory result is obtained as there is no scheduling element and resource costing tends to be constrained within rather inflexible rules. In relatively small networks it is probably quicker to make a manual calculation. Chapter 6 will explore the problems of using a fully integrated computer system which includes costing.

These preliminary activity costs can now be brought together into one total for the project. Separate calculations must also be made of all the indirect costs such as project management and administration and any other items not specifically allocated to activities but still directly related to the project. Some provision should also be made for contingencies. These indirect costs are also totalled and expressed as a preliminary percentage of direct costs.

It is very unlikely that the sum of direct and indirect costs calculated in this way will be equal to the desired project value and it is now necessary to bring the two totals into balance. This leads to a progressive review of the resource requirements of activities and the proposed method of working; it might be unrealistic to adjust every item in the project by a fixed

Alloc'n No.	Description	First Estimate	Second Estimate	Final Estimate
	Direct activity costs			
	General costs			
	Total			

General cost as % of total—

	1st estimate	
	2nd estimate	
	final estimate	

Budget figure:	Prepared by
	Checked by
Contingency included in budget:	Date

Fig. 2.7   Cost estimating summary sheet

percentage in order to achieve the required balance—many items will contain firm cost estimates which can certainly not be cut and are not likely to be exceeded in practice. There is therefore a certain limit to the range of adjustments to the initial activity costs, beyond which the overall project budget sum has to be called into question.

It is now necessary to plot from the initial activity resource lists and schedule, the preliminary total demand for each type of resource in each time period as shown in Fig. 2.8.

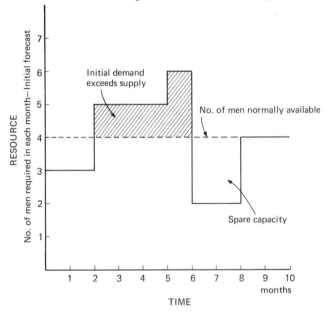

Fig. 2.8   Calculating resource demands indicated during activity cost estimating

Even though at this stage no resource levelling has been carried out and the resource demands have been plotted by early start, visual inspection of the resulting plot will indicate the approximate overload in relation to estimated levels of availability. A preliminary judgement will probably be made about the significance of indicated resource overloads. If these are mainly related to manpower forecasts they can in some cases be ironed out at this stage by allowing for the cost of the necessary overtime working or by reviewing the earlier activity duration estimate and resource requirement.

Proposed costs must take into account these and other similar variations in resource requirements and uncertainties in other resource forecasts. Questions may also need to be asked about the assumptions made in fixing resource levels. In many cases these are in fact flexible and depend as much upon the state of the market and the techniques and know-how in the business as upon the total budget. Any cuts needed in the initial cost estimates must take account of all these factors, particularly the interpretation of indicated "loading" for each time period.

2.06 Adjusting resource requirements to "match" the desired project value

The balancing process involves a certain philosophy: that the project should employ resources in the most efficient manner. This implies that techniques must be developed to a reliability level which prevents waste during the project. The less well-tested and proven the techniques, the higher the risk of an eventual cost over-run. This point must be carefully borne in mind as there is often a conflict of objectives in highly sophisticated organisations between project efficiency and professional or academic requirements. This conflict should be kept carefully under review and in the balancing process the opportunity should be taken to examine proposed technical methods more carefully.

The project manager must bear in mind the balance needed in the project between the use of new techniques with their high risk element and longer established methods. The decision on this balance is probably the most difficult and important in the whole project planning process. Having decided what techniques should be employed, it may be necessary to examine further methods of achieving the required balance. For instance, on review complete activities may be cut out, although it is more likely that the more economical use of resources will provide the bulk of any necessary savings. A possible approach to this cost saving process is set out in Fig. 2.9.

The traditional networking approach is to cut back critical activities. This may be quite successful but should only be one of a series of investigations which are carried out to highlight the real problems of uncertainty, inflation or high cost traditional methods. These are common to the oldest established project industries such as ship building. In such industries, where competition is fierce, the risks of loss are

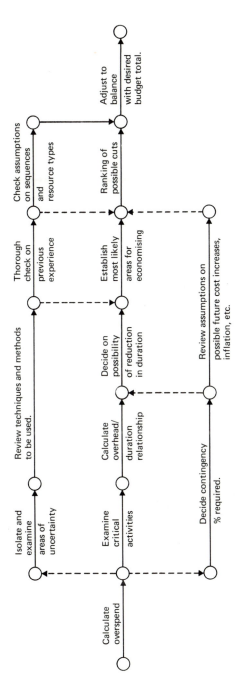

Fig. 2.9 Possible approach to budget balancing process

relatively great and one of the key questions for the United Kingdom in the 1970s is whether to under-write these risks in aircraft manufacture, mining, ship building and even in computer manufacturing. To these industries the techniques being described are of the utmost importance.

Later examples will illustrate the application of this cutting back procedure in particular circumstances. The reader must remember however that the cutting back is at the cost forecasting stage of an established contract or project. In this sense it implies that the contract sum or project value has been agreed on the basis of often rather "rushed" estimating in which there may not be time to study the more detailed implications. The project manager's real problem therefore at this stage is to produce a project plan which will, when all the resources and costs are taken into account, produce the required profit to cover the costs of finance (in 1970 running between 10% and 15% per annum) and to provide the risk-taking equity shareholders with a reasonable return on their investment. On top of this it also has to ensure the viability of the business with provision for taxation, replacement of equipment, and any other reserves peculiar to the type of business.

Having decided on the best method of reducing planned levels of spending, and agreed these with management (and with the client where necessary) the project manager can adjust the sums available for each activity, calculate the total overhead and spread this over all activities. The format in Fig. 2.7 is designed for this purpose, and Fig. 2.10 shows an example of the process.

2.07 Resource levelling/Cost schedules

Resource levelling, which is the art of adjusting the sequence of events to make the best use of resources without gaps or overlaps, can be done either manually or with the aid of a computer. In our experience with (purposely) small control networks it has been best to leave the resource runs on the computer (for example RPSM, PERT, etc..) until after the stage of levelling, using the computer programs mainly to calculate and provide:

1 Scheduled starts (i.e. after resource levelling)
2 Convenient documents for all departments or individuals concerned in the project
3 Resource utilisation data.

COST ESTIMATING SUMMARY SHEET			Sheet .... of	
PROJECT: *(name of project)*			NUMBER: *125*	

Alloc'n No.	Description	First Estimate	Second Estimate	Final Estimate
	Direct activity costs			
011	*Prelims*	*600*	*590*	*590*
012	*Zone plan*	*200*	*200*	*180*
013	*Street index*	*450*	*450*	*410*
014	*Census data*	*450*		
021	*Design*		*400*	*320*
	...ct polidride survey	*1,650*	*1,650*	*1,650*
070	*Cederondride survey*	*1,800*	*1,800*	*1,720*
080	*Analyse and report*	*1,700*	*1,500*	*1,270*
	Total	*7,920*	*7,285*	*6,560*
	General costs			
200	*General direction*	*520*	*425*	*400*
205	*General data analysis*	*310*	*310*	*290*
	Contingency	*200*	*100*	*—*
	Total	*1,030*	*835*	*690*
	Total	*8,950*	*8,120*	*7,250*

General cost as % of total—	1st estimate	*11·7*	
	2nd estimate	*10·3*	
	final estimate	*9·5*	

Budget figure:	*7,250*	Prepared by	
		Checked by	
Contingency included in budget:	*—*	Date	

Fig. 2.10 Example of the process of balancing the budget

This may seem at first sight to be the wrong sequence, but unfortunately no available computer software can at this stage give more than an indication of resource/cost over-run. Even if the resource runs are carried out sooner, the project manager is still left with the problem of sifting through the different alternative methods of cost saving. Where, however, suitable computing capacity is freely available within the organisation, and a large project is in hand, then it is necessary for the project manager to study the specification of relevant computer programs to ascertain which can be:

1 Most economically used for cost forecasting
2 Used to input resource/cost data on a realistic basis
3 Used to effect resource levelling calculations (preferably with output showing resource demand levels by time period).

In our approach, we are now suggesting that the project manager should input resource data after satisfying himself that the total resource costs, including overheads and the profit element, are within the budget. He must therefore proceed either by manual computation or by computer program calculations to produce lists of activities by "scheduled" start. (*Scheduled start* is a technical term which implies that the activity has been phased to take account of resource loadings, and that resource levelling has been achieved.) When complete, these are used as input to the activity cost form.

2.08 Resource Data—Input/Output

The process of resource data input is quite straightforward, involving:

1 Listing of resource types to be scheduled
2 Allocation of a code number to each resource
3 Calculation of adjusted resource requirements by activity
4 Completion of resource columns on activity data sheets
5 Decisions about available resource levels by time period
6 The overall duration of the project.

This information is input on standard punching instruction sheets where each horizontal line represents an activity. Resource types (recognised by code letter or number), resource levels, time units, duration and required output are all specified on the sheet. Manual or computer calculation then provides complete schedules of work showing forecast start date for each activity, the planned duration and the relationship with other activities. This is a most important document, which is often printed out into separate schedules for each resource, person, or department as appropriate to the project in hand. Fig. 2.11 shows part of a typical schedule of this type.

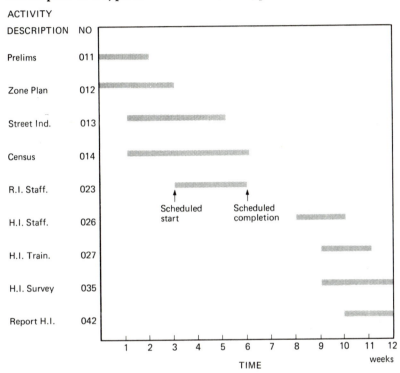

Note: This type of chart is an extract from the Project Plan which shows the schedule for one type of resource and highlights times of overlapping and "gaps" in the schedule

Fig. 2.11 Typical bar chart for one resource type—by scheduled start date

2.09 Establishment of related accounts procedures

(i) Administrative procedures

It is in this area that the utmost co-operation is needed between the central accounting and administrative departments and the project manager, unless the project manager is himself in a position to be able to collect, code and analyse his own project costs. Certain problems arise particularly when setting up an integrated costing and operational control system for the first time:

1 The coding and allocation of actual staff costs to activities during the course of the project
2 The coding and recording of "transactions"—for example, invoices received from suppliers of materials or other services used in the project
3 The time lag between spending (i.e. "use" in the activity sense) and the receipt of invoices from suppliers
4 The time needed for data processing
5 The speed with which information is needed to be effective (We consider that, for a typical review cycle of one month this time should ideally be no more than five working days.)
6 The link between project transaction allocation and the preparation of accounts to be sent to the client
7 The need to keep those records which are required for standard accounting and auditing purposes (quarterly and annual trading account and balance sheets).

Project cost accounting tends to cut across some of these basic accounting requirements. It calls therefore for a special effort. Where a company carries out most of its business in the form of projects it should seriously consider converting any budgeting or costing system on to an activity base. This does not prevent the necessary item code analysis of costs required for annual accounts—for example telephone, rent, salaries, wages, data processing, rentals and so on. These can be "captured", listed and recorded as part of a data processing routine.

In order to make a start with this problem the following steps are needed:

1 To specify the cost accounting requirements
2 To agree procedural arrangements for coding, recording and verification of data.

In the following paragraphs we describe a computerised activity cost-accounting system which we have found effective. Its development required very close co-operation between the financial heads of operations in the organisation to make sure that the interests and requirements of each were met. The essential requirements of its routines were that it should accept the following inputs:

1 A list of all resources, suitably coded and described in a semi-permanent file
2 A list of all resource costs linked to '1', giving all salaries and emoluments of all professional and technical staff in the organisation, together with the appropriate factors for converting these to "sales value" rates
3 A list of all project numbers, both prefix and suffix, forming a semi-permanent file of activity cost numbers and descriptions
4 The monthly resource utilisation by project/activity number
5 The monthly list of transactions in money terms, both debit and credit, and their activity and item codes in suitable resource units.

The computer program analyses the monthly inputs of resource usage and transactions and, by applying the appropriate rates to each resource, calculates the monthly cost of resources used by each activity. These are then listed by activity number providing a sub-total for each main resource and an ordered listing with sub-totals for transactions by item code. Individual activity costs are printed on sequential sheets and are summed for the project, the summary containing all total activity costs and all item codes listed and summed.

The program accepts input relating to all current projects simultaneously and provides separate summaries for each project and a combined summary for the whole organisation. Thus the program prints out monthly total actual cost and the total receivable income for each activity for each project for the whole range of projects within the organisation. The value of such an analysis is immense if prepared quickly after the end of each month.

(Detail relating to the program specification can be made available, suitably modified for the needs of individual organisations, from Computation, Research and Development Limited; a similar program is provided on a commercial basis by Honeywell through their Bureaux.)

It may take a considerable time to work up such a tailor-made program through initial specification, writing, testing, correcting and refining. This will obviously not be viable for an individual project unless it is extremely large. It must be carried out as a matter of company philosophy and must cover all the project activities of the company. For an individual project the choice lies between manual methods of allocation and calculation (not too great a task) or the use of bureau services. The output from the program links directly with the need of the project manager for actual activity costs and income by month; these can be entered on to the activity cost sheet and the monthly project report form and compared with the project budget, thus permitting a realistic overall assessment of progress in the project.

(ii) Accounts and Administration

We have already referred to the question of project and activity cost numbering in an earlier section. It can be assumed that the accounting function will allocate the basic project code number and will accept from the project manager his list of activity code numbers and descriptions. Having agreed this code numbering system a way must be devised to ensure that all costs are properly allocated to the correct number. This calls for the coding and authorisation of transactions and agreement about sequencing of returns, and the completion of monthly time sheets by members of staff with allocation of time directed to numbered activities. In order to make this work, the preparation of the list of activity numbers must be accompanied by the proper briefing of all staff members involved in the project and of members of the staff of the accounting section of the firm.

Two problems are likely to arise in this area of operations:

1 Communication between the accounts department and the project manager
2 The time base of transactions

In order to iron out the first problem in our own case, we worked closely together to establish a routine for the authorisation of invoices and the verification of time sheets. In the case of invoices from suppliers, these are seen by accountants as "accounts payable" and should be posted direct to the appropriate ledger. The same invoices are seen by the project manager as activity costs and must be coded as such. All accounts are therefore passed direct to the project manager for

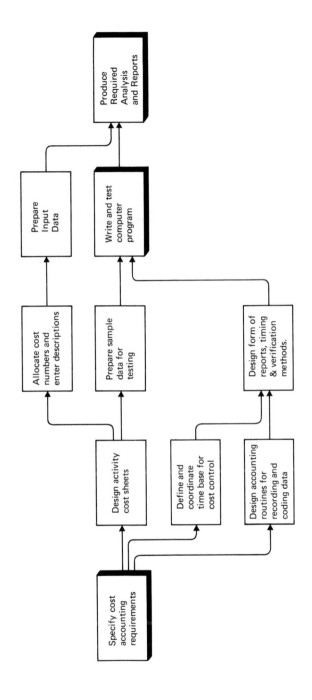

Fig. 2.12 Essential steps in liaison between the project manager and the accounting and administration group

authorisation and allocation, using a simple rubber stamp which helps to make sure that all the necessary information is recorded on the original invoice. The invoice is then passed back to the accounts department for the necessary book entries and cost analysis. Because such invoices form part of the auditable records of the company, their treatment and filing has to serve a dual purpose at the accounting end.

The first problem impinges upon the second, that of the time base for cost accounting. A further agreement on procedure must be thrashed out. From the project control point of view it is better to account for commitments as soon as they are incurred rather than when invoices are received or even when invoices are paid. If the project manager wants to know where he really stands he must take account of his expenditure on the project at the moment when the materials or services are actually supplied; however, there is some danger in using suppliers' estimates, because they may not coincide precisely with the actual invoice when this is submitted probably a month later. The best compromise is to account for invoices received and not for commitments. The accounting month can be staggered by one or even two weeks from the cost control month-end, so as to allow a reasonable time for the data processing and checking of transactions without delaying the production of the monthly cost control records. This means that the cost control records are not precise, but the amount of error is not likely to be great and is in any case self-correcting as time goes by.

The other way of dealing with transactions would be to record them only when invoices were actually paid, as is done in simple book-keeping practice. While this gives the actual cash position at any given time it is almost useless for the purpose of cost control of a live project. It is quite common for as much as three months credit to be taken on accounts received and the distortion of the true committed state of the project can be imagined. While it can be argued that the project manager should keep such a close eye on events within the project that he can make suitable adjustments to the output from the accounting procedure, experience shows that it is only too easy for costs to escalate without proper information and control and it is only through adopting a coherent system such as the one described above that an ordered review of progress can be achieved.

(iii) Training the staff involved

It may seem obvious in setting up a new system that particular attention should be given to the training of the staff involved. We believe that this should be carried out by a combination of on-the-job training, staff briefing and a study of the communication requirements of the individual concerned.

Thus all project staff who will need to use activity cost numbers must be briefed on the whole project, using the control base network, and the significance of the activity suffix numbers must be emphasised. Staff must accept the idea of time sheets as providing essential project analysis data, particularly where hours worked in professional organisations are the basis for the income of the business.

Appropriate lists of activities and their code numbers must therefore be readily available to all staff.

The project office manager must be thoroughly briefed on all these procedures, and if he is accountant trained he may have to modify his traditional approach. His function is to act as the link between the accounts department and the technical project management and he must be given instruction and training in the preparation of activity cost accounting methods. He must take the responsibility for collecting and collating all necessary cost data each month and for processing it quickly and efficiently.

Staff in the accounts department must make an attempt to become familiar with the concepts of activities within projects. They should be briefed on the project as a whole and given an understanding of the method of control to be adopted and its importance to their organisation. Accounts staff will have to learn how to transcribe invoice and cost data to coding sheets for processing by the computer and will have to build up working relationships with computer personnel.

Above all, it is essential that one man is given the responsibility to press forward with the preparation each month of the project cost accounts. This requires initiative and assistance in gathering data which, however well processed, is of maximum use only when it is processed very quickly and presented to the project manager in a way which will allow him to take account of it in the running of his project. Such a system demands a high level of inter-departmental co-operation. In the real world this is often difficult to achieve but great benefits are lost to the organisation if a determined and sustained effort is not made to establish the necessary routine and to maintain it through time.

This chapter has been concerned with the way in which the project manager and his organisation can initiate a system of cost forecasting and cost accounting which will provide the management information which he needs to control the profitability of his project. It has discussed procedures, systems, data processing, forecasting, accounting and costing. These and others are the essential elements of our system, which will be illustrated by practical situations in the following chapters.

Part two - Case studies

3 Simple manual methods

3.01 Introduction

There must be hundreds of organisations in which small and medium sized projects are handled by trained and experienced personnel who probably do not think that anyone could tell them anything about how to run their jobs. This is particularly the case when the project is of such a size that the project manager can handle it with a small team and without delegating much responsibility.

We think, however, there are many such cases where a system of network planning and cost control can be applied in a simple way very much to the advantage both of the project manager and of his directors. This chapter takes as an example of such a project a study carried out by the Scottish Division of Freeman, Fox and Associates into the future road pattern of an area in central Scotland based on the Burghs of Falkirk and Grangemouth.

The characteristics of this study which make it a useful example include:

(i) *The size of the project team.* The project manager is supported by two or three technical assistants in Scotland and is served by other specialist assistants such as computer personnel, data analysts, economists and drawing office staff, all of whom have other projects to serve at the same time

(ii) *The split locality of the study.* The work originates in and is controlled from Scotland but, at certain stages, much of it is actually carried out on the computer in

London

(iii) *Budget limitations.* The Client for whom the study is undertaken has expressed his determination that the study shall not exceed its cost estimate

(iv) *Possible changes to the study programme.* Although the project has been defined fairly precisely it is in the nature of work like this that new and better ideas develop as the study unfolds. It is often necessary, therefore, to change the project plan and budget to accommodate these.

Thus the project has all the ingredients needed to justify a planning and cost control system but its scale does not demand the "full treatment" and manual methods of applying the basic principles will be sufficient.

3.02 Description of the project

Although for the purpose of this book it is not necessary to go into detail on all aspects of the project, which is somewhat specialised, we think that a general description of what is involved will help to illustrate the planning and control procedure.

Falkirk and Grangemouth are adjacent towns mid-way between Glasgow and Edinburgh. Between them they occupy a strategic position in the development of central Scotland with road, rail and sea communications giving ready access to the rest of Britain and the continent. The area has been part of larger regional land use and transportation studies in recent years and as a result of these a tentative future road pattern has been drawn up by the local authorities and Government departments concerned.

The objectives of the present study are to look in more detail at the forecasts of population and employment for the area; to predict the likely pattern of travel demand in ten and twenty years time; and to make estimates of how the proposed new road system would cope with the demand.

The techniques for this type of study are quite complex, but in essence they consist of collecting information about the present-day pattern of travel movements, and establishing relationships between the socio/economic chatacteristics of the area and the travel patterns which result from them. The relationships are stated in the form of a mathematical model for which the use of a computer is essential. The next step is to forecast changes in socio/economic factors ten and twenty years ahead—changes in population, changes in type of employment and numbers of people employed and changes in "real" income. Using these forecasts the model is able to predict the likely future travel demand pattern which can be applied to the various road schemes to see whether they are likely to be adequate.

Fig. 3.1 shows a simple "landscape" network showing the main elements of the study.

All the techniques and computer programs for the study have been developed, tested and used in previous studies so that there is plenty of information available on which to base cost estimates and from which to draw experience so that, from an organisation point of view, this could be described as a straightforward project of its type.

We would not like the reader to form the impression that such work is in any sense dull, however. A great deal is demanded of the project team and they are very well aware that the results of their work will be used in one form or another in the development of the area, with real consequences in human terms.

3.03 Management purposes

In our example, the project manager needs a system which will do the following:

1 Allow him to appreciate present and future problems of management and control
2 To communicate, for example to describe the project to his client, his directors and his own team
3 To coordinate activities in Scotland and London in order that deadlines can be met
4 To motivate the activities of specialists to fit in with his programme requirements in the most economical fashion
5 To plan the study budget
6 To exercise management control so that the project is completed in time and in accordance with its budget, and incidentally produces a satisfactory profit.

In addition, senior management needs a system which can produce quickly and reasonably accurately a clear statement

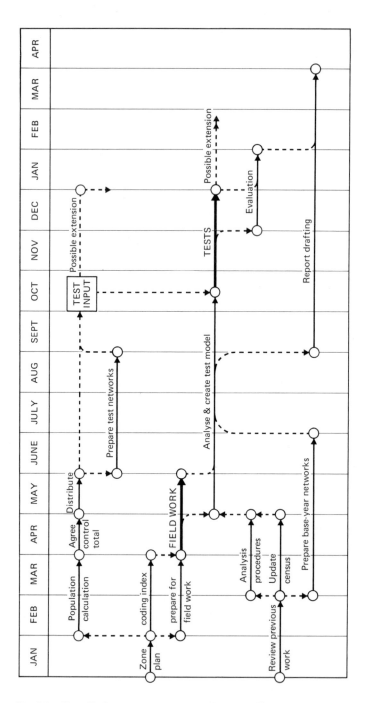

Fig. 3.1   Simplified project network—the "landscape"

MAY			JUNE				JULY					AUGUST				SEPTEMBER				OCTOBER				N
15	22	29	5	12	19	26	3	10	17	24	31	7	14	21	28	4	11	18	25	2	9	16	23	30	6	13

1991c Network (163)

1981 and 1981b Networks (161, 163)

1991 tests and with client (7, 163) (Test and Evaluate 1991c Network P) (138, 161, 162)

calculate 1991/Submittal (134) *Run 1981 site* (134) *Do 1981 test* (134) (133) *Evaluate 1981 test and discuss with client* (141, 162)

Detailed 1981 Economic Evaluation (163)

Current Situation *1991 Tests* (180) *1981 Tests* (180) *Finish Report* (180)

Paper on 1991 Evaluation *Meeting on 1991 Evaluation* *Paper on 1981 Test results* *Meeting on 1981 Test results*

each month of the progress of the work in terms both of time and money, together with the means of identifying any parts of the project which may go wrong so that action can be taken to remedy this.

3.04 The project network

The pattern of this study—the sequence of events and the nature of the events themselves—is similar to that of many previous studies. This, and the fact that the size of the study is not large in comparative terms, means that the project network can be built up quite simply on the basis of previous experience. Some aspects of the timetable are dependent upon seasonal considerations, for instance, field work for this type of survey must be at the "average" time of the year so that this activity is fixed in the calendar and the preceding and succeeding activities have to fit with it. Thus a simplified project network, the landscape, can be established without difficulty and can act as the framework of the more complicated project control network.

Fig. 3.1 shows the simplified project network for this particular study, indicating the main elements in relation to one another and also showing the possible extensions of the study if, in due course, these are required by the client.

All the main items shown in this landscape network are standard practice. By reference to the work done in previous studies, the activities may now be listed in detail; then by constant cross-referencing between the landscape network and the activity list the project engineer can draw up the project control network. Fig. 3.2 illustrates this network.

In this case the engineer has found it convenient to draw the network directly in the form of a bar chart, and the links between activities have been omitted although they can be detected by examination. In this case the engineer has used the traditional format for project control and, because of the relative simplicity of the project, he has been able to draw it *ab initio*. In the more complex projects described in later chapters it will be seen that the bar chart is produced by the computer from the original logic diagram or network.

The network contains all the activities in the list and shows their cost allocation numbers, thus making it easy for staff working on the project to identify the work they are doing on their personal records.

3.05 The project budget

In what might be described in management terms as a routine project of intermediate size, there are generally sufficient experience and good enough cost records available from past studies to enable an approximate budget to be calculated on the basis of likely staff involvement and likely expenses. The time-scale of the project is known from the project network so that the first budget calculation can be made very simply as indicated in Fig. 3.3. The reader should note that for obvious reasons of confidentiality, the names, rates and other figures in this example have been omitted, and the pro-forma is included merely to illustrate the principles of the method.

A separate approach to the budget is now made on a rather more systematic basis. The list of activities in the project has been taken from the cost control records of previous studies so that there is direct comparability between the different parts of each study. Thus each activity can be compared in its likely size and duration with the similar activity in previous studies, and an individual estimate can be made of its likely cost. In the present case, the number of roadside interview stations can be compared with the number of stations in some other study. An assessment can be made of the relative traffic intensities and the previous cost records can then be used as the basis for estimating.

This process is repeated for each activity in the list and the total of the individual estimates is compared with the total obtained from the first, staff-based estimate. The two are then brought into balance by applying commonsense and experience so that the result is a complete list of activities each with its own budget, together with a corresponding breakdown of the budget based on staff involvement and likely expenses. The only resource scheduling likely to be needed in a project of this size will be to check that the required staff will in fact be available at the times they are needed in the project. This will have been kept in mind during the build up of the network and the budget so that no problem is likely to arise here.

The next task is to break down each individual budget into estimates of likely monthly expenditure, based upon the activity durations shown on the project network. From this it is

Name of Project:
    Preliminary Budget Estimate by Staff & Expense Schedule

1. STAFF COSTS (SALES VALUE)

Name	Monthly Charging rate	No. of months involvement	amount

Total direct staff charges   :
Add allowance for salary charges   :
Add cost of Directors attending
meetings   :

Total estimated manpower cost   :

2. OUT-OF-POCKET EXPENSES (AT COST)
            Travelling and subsistence   :
            Computer   :
            Miscellaneous   :

            Total   :

3. CONTINGENCY SUM   :
            Total cost estimate   :

Fig. 3.3 Example of preliminary budget estimate

a simple matter to produce a likely monthly expenditure curve.

It should be noted in passing that for this type of project in Great Britain the cost control basis is the "sales value" based upon the standard scales of hourly charges for staff.

3.06 Administrative procedures

In order to maintain cost control certain very simple administrative procedures must be accomplished each month. Circulation of the project network to all members of staff concerned in the project showing cost allocation numbers is an essential starting point. These numbers are used in the recording of staff time on daily, weekly or monthly time sheets which have to be analysed to produce the estimate of actual cost. At the same time, expenses which are chargeable to the project are allocated to their correct suffix number by the project manager as the invoices come in from various suppliers. Such expenses include, for instance, the cost of police supervision of roadside interview stations, allocated directly to the roadside interview survey, and the costs of running the computer, allocated to the relevant number, and also the travel costs.

At the end of each month all the activity costs are calculated. These include some general items such as general direction, not otherwise allocated directly to suffixes but nevertheless a charge to the project. Such charges are distributed among the directly allocated charges each month in a systematic manner by the project manager. We think it quite important that he should have the task of doing this as it may be that a strict mathematical distribution of these charges would give a distorted picture of actual costs. One might, for instance, get the case of a very expensive item such as the printing out of roadside interview survey tabulations in one month, an item which might have required almost no supervision apart from that of the data analyst who has allocated his time directly to it. It would be unfair for the cost of general direction to be added to this with the same weight as to other, more staff-intensive activities.

These perfectly straightforward administrative tasks should not take more than a few days after the end of each month and these can provide the project manager with the basis for his cost control and for his management report.

3.07 Management report and cost control

We have found that the management report summary illustrated in Fig. 1.3 provides a very effective tool both for cost control and for the information of top management on the progress of a project. Fig. 3.4 shows one or two typical extracts from a management report based upon the present example.

This shows that item 133 began about one month late, has caught up with its original programme and is likely to be completed for something less than its original budget, whereas the entire project is running a little behind its schedule and, because the value of work done appears to be slightly less than the amount spent, the implication is that the final cost will be somewhat higher than the original budget. This sort of information can be used initially by the project manager to regulate the intensity of effort in the study in order to maintain balance. It can also be used by top management to decide whether the project is far enough out of balance financially to warrant approaching the client to warn him of a likely change in the budget.

3.08 Value of the method

The reader will see that in this example we have used much of the basic theory expressed in Chapters One and Two but in a very simplified manner. We think that this is entirely appropriate for the scale of project described and that the amount of work involved in setting up the cost control system and keeping it going is amply re-paid by the production of the resulting information regularly and promptly. In particular, staff at all levels in the project can see the effect of speeding up or slowing down their own part in the project and, as they are liable to be working on several other projects at the same time, this is particularly useful in maintaining progress.

It can be seen, however, that the system described is only really suitable for individuals working on quite small projects. As soon as one tries to extend it to cover a number of simultaneous projects it is obvious that the manual analysis of data will become a much larger task and it is at this stage that one should begin to consider the use of a computer in the cost control process.

PROJECT NO.
Grangemouth/Falkirk Growth Area Road Study.

POSITION AT END OF JUNE 1971

		To End Feb	MARCH	APRIL	MAY	JUNE	JULY	AUG	SEPT	OCT	TOTAL BUDGET	AMOUNT SPENT	% SP.	% COMP.	VALUE OF WORK DONE	REMARKS
133 Code employment Survey data	B		100	250	450	450	100				1350			95	1280	ahead and inside budget
	A			272	390	420						1082	88			
134 check and edit e.s. data	B			50	50	150	150	50			450			20	90	O.K.
	A					72						72	16			
135 Tabulate e.s. data	B							150			150					
	A							150								
136 Code parking data	B															
	A															
TOTALS	B	1020	1450	1620	2590	2840					19020				16330	Running a little late and a little over-spent.
	A											17518				

Fig. 3.4 Monthly summary report to management

4 More advanced method - an example based on a large planning study

4.01 Introduction

In 1966, when the authors first met, we had been developing our interests in project control in different ways. Each of us was, however, concerned with the problem of planning and controlling projects for profit. Our joint concern was to apply such techniques as were available to this end in the field of land use and transportation planning, an emergent science, which, in the United Kingdom at any rate, had until then been much more a matter of research than one of business. Our concern in planning for profit was dual:

1 To enable the firm to prosper in a business sense
2 To obtain and retain a name for reliability and efficiency which would ensure long-term goodwill and give value for money to our clients.

In order to do this successfully, it was necessary to develop better methods of estimating, better definitions of work content and methods of control. These improvements obviously depended on better management information and the planning and cost control system, which the authors developed can, therefore, be termed a "management information system".

This chapter describes how we worked together to develop the system on an actual project of some magnitude and shows how far we found we were able to take our ideas at that stage.

4.02 The estimating process

Our first step was to produce a network of basic activities

describing the work content of the project. Producing this
initial document was in itself a fundamental advance in our
thinking, although we now recognise the network as a very
crude first attempt. This network has been reproduced in
Fig. 4.1.

This network was itself based upon the compilation of a list
of all the basic activities which could be foreseen at that stage.
It should be explained that this was done at the inception of the
project. The client, the Scottish Development Department, had
asked us, and several other firms of consultants, to suggest a
method of tackling the problem of how to estimate the regional
consequences of a variety of planning and transport proposals
covering the next twenty years. This stage of the project could
then be described, in business terms, as the pre-contract or
tender phase, although it must be emphasised that consultants
do not compete with one another on the basis of price in the
same way as contractors, and the competition was to produce a
well-founded programme of work required to answer the
problem, with a target completion date and within a reasonable
estimate of cost.

Information on the details of the project were incomplete at
this stage and the isolation of uncertainties in certain areas of
the work was a significant outcome of the exercise of listing
activities and drawing the network. The list included forty-six
basic activities ranging from setting up the project office
through the design and conduct of the various surveys, the
analysis of survey data, the prediction of future changes in
social and travel patterns, to the testing of various transport
proposals, the evaluation of the results and the drafting of the
final report. These forty-six basic activities were the project
manager's first attempt to establish the content of the work.
For each activity a preliminary estimate of duration and
manpower requirements was made. The following example
shows the appropriate depth of consideration given at this stage
of the process:

"Activity Number 26: *Cordon and screenline roadside
surveys.* Some eighty roads are cut by the tentative screen
and cordon lines. On each of these there will be one weekday
of interviewing and one whole week of automatic traffic
counting. Each team needs a supervisor and five assistants,
together with equipment, transport, etc. Thus the whole

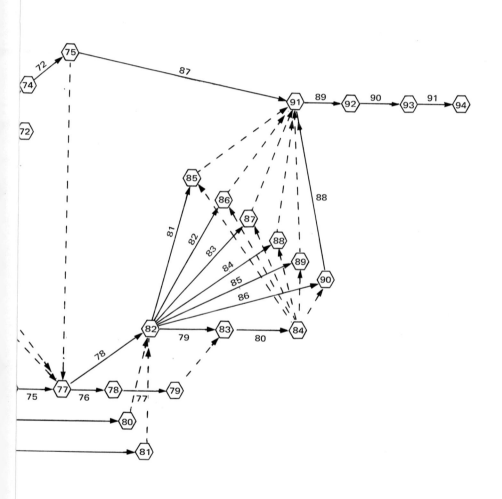

activity for eighty stations needs four teams for forty working days, with an allowance for possible adverse weather conditions."

A schedule of such activity descriptions was circulated for discussion and comment to all the senior staff involved. In this way the combined knowledge and experience of carrying out similar projects which had been built up in the United Kingdom through the London Transportation Study and the West Midlands Transport Study were brought to bear. These techniques were in a stage of rapid development at the time, with the emergence of improved software* and the application of mathematical models to predict the growth in car ownership and travel generally. These developments in themselves posed a considerable problem because the precise specification of the information to be collected in surveys depended upon the software to be used. Thus early decisions had to be made on the overall approach to be applied and the amount of programming which would be required. Thus the simple exercise of listing activities and drawing a network was already identifying decision points and crystallising the study programme.

Consultation with other members of the firm's staff produced amendments to the first list and a good many additions to it. This resulted in a revised and more complex network which is reproduced in Fig. 4.2.

4.03 Improved definitions of work content

Detailed discussions then ensued and, through a series of amendments, detailed activity-based cost estimates were evolved. Once again it should be emphasised that these cost estimates were not produced for the purpose of tendering but merely, at this stage, in order to make sure that the technical proposal put to the client would not, if accepted, turn out to be unreasonably expensive.

Through this internal consultative procedure, which took place over a period of several weeks prior to presenting technical proposals to the client, the various problem areas were progressively brought under a "microscope", isolating areas of greatest uncertainty and in which further definition would be required before a final cost estimate was produced.

* software: computer programs specially written for particular problems

This estimating process was probably little different in intensity from the normal procedures. The important and significant point about it was the intention to apply it as the basis for a management control system in which costing was linked directly to project activities and a project network. This intention was stimulated by the general feeling that land use transportation studies had gone through a long enough period of research unencumbered by financial considerations, and by the realisation that this project was the ideal opportunity for introducing some form of systematic control. For this purpose a budgetary limit was imposed and the early estimates went through a series of refinements, fitting the technical considerations to the overall financial constraints. This process created a ceiling on experimentation and forced management decisions about economy in methods and in use of resources.

Estimating by activity was found to be significantly different from estimating by function, operation or type of resource. It was more difficult, as it demanded greater attention to the actual method to be employed to perform each activity. In doing this it led to a clarification of the general methods of land use and transportation planning and it certainly isolated the key problem areas and drew them to the attention of management.

Fig. 4.2, the Project Network and Staff Schedule, was eventually used in the presentation of the technical proposal to the client to illustrate the sequence of operations in the study and to point out the key dates for decisions and actions. The staff schedule shown on this drawing was built up from an analysis of the preliminary staffing estimates for each of the activities, and the overall duration of the project was estimated by tracing the critical path through the network. We think it true to say that the presentation of this information to the client was a material factor in the decision to invite the firm to carry out the study, thus demonstrating the usefulness of network planning as a means of communication, in this case explaining how we would go about the job and showing that we had a good basis for stating how long we thought it would take to complete and how many people we would need to complete it.

4.04 Creation of the project control system

Once the firm had received the commission for the project the tentative budget ceiling became the official budget and the project manager had to set about the task of reworking the basic activity resource estimates with detailed costing and balancing to produce the control system.

The first step in this process was to firm up the network as a fully agreed procedural basis of working, as uncertainty still remained at that stage in certain parts of the work. However, even though the procedure was agreed it was thought wise to allow a contingency item to cover unexpected costs. This should always be done as something extra is usually needed.

Notwithstanding the contingency sum, the budget available for each activity was purposely kept as tight as possible and it became evident that key personnel would have to be most carefully briefed to ensure that they followed the agreed methods. Certain activities in the programming and data processing fields were notorious sources of over-spending, and particular efforts were needed initially and during the project to keep these within the time and cost limits set. It was, of course, recognised from the outset that there would be large variations between the plan and the actual performance for individual activities, particularly as the firm had not attempted cost forecasting on a systematic basis previously and there was not much recorded evidence on which to base the estimates for each activity. Even so the project manager expected such variations to be self-compensating, and regarded the contingency sum as a reserve for the most extreme situations.

The 'project plan' in its final form consisted of ninety-seven activities with an overall duration of twenty months and an overall budget, including the contingency item, of £167,000. The first step towards integrating this operational plan with the budgetary control system was to allocate a cost number to each activity. The project itself was also allocated a code number—623. Reference numbers were to be used through the project, but were built up at that stage in flexible groupings to allow for amendments and additions as the project progressed. Having embarked on what was to us a new technique, we decided at this point to use the computer to analyse the network. The basic activity data with amended time estimates were prepared for computing using the then CEIR CPM program*. The input to this program was restricted to activities, their agreed logical sequence as defined by the I J of the start

* CEIR is now known as SCICON Limited: CPM stands for critical path method

and end nodes, the estimated duration and the resource requirements. No resource scheduling was required and activity resource requirements were input in order that they should appear on the bar chart print-out. The coding facilities in CPM were used for this purpose. Fig. 4.3 shows a sample of the input.

The schedule was specified in units of weeks in order to obtain a bar chart for the total project duration. The print-out was to be a listing by earliest start. In effect, the project was originally scheduled to start on 31st January 1967 and to finish in August 1968. The time limit had been established from a manual analysis to find the critical path and overall duration.

Figs. 4.4 and 4.5 reproduce parts of the actual print-out. The complete print-out was in bar chart form consisting of all ninety-seven activities. This covered five separate sheets of output and was used throughout the project as the overall management control chart.

It can be seen that the print-out did not include cost allocation numbers which were added subsequently for ease of identification. Also, certain alterations were made to activity descriptions and other data during the course of the study.

The importance of this bar chart at the start of the project, showing earliest start times and available float for each activity, lay not so much in computing these items which could have been done equally well manually, but in providing an easily usable scheduling sheet with which the project manager could programme the use of his resources. Figs. 4.4 and 4.5 show the way in which the timings indicated in the print-out were amended when resource calculations were carried out.

This scheduling process was carried out for each key resource by printing out an individual bar chart of the activities which used it. Individual bar charts were produced for each key member of the team and for the groups of temporary field and office workers. Altogether eleven such individual charts were printed-out. Fig. 4.6 shows the bar chart for the senior planner and the way in which the demand for his service through the period of the contract was calculated. The process of adjusting activity timing to take account of these individual resource loadings was carried out manually. The resultant times for starting and finishing activities were then marked up on the master control chart as shown in Figs. 4.4 and 4.5.

I	J	DURATION (D)	TARGET START (TS)	TARGET COMPLETION (TC)	M or D	C	ACTIVITY DESCRIPTION (SORT, SKIP & SUPPRESS CODES IN CC 21-50 ONLY)	S or T T	RESOURCE 1		RESOURCE 2		RESOURCE 3		RESOURCE 4	
									TYPE	QUANTITY	TYPE	QUANTITY	TYPE	Q'NTY	TYPE	Q'NTY
1	2	6	0				SET UP OFFICE	L	I	P	I					

Column positions (card columns): I = 1-4; J = 5-8; DURATION (D) = 9-12; TARGET START (TS) = 13-16; TARGET COMPLETION (TC) = 17-20; M or D = 21; C = 22; ACTIVITY DESCRIPTION = 23-61; S or T T = 62-63; RESOURCE 1 TYPE 63, QUANTITY 64-67; RESOURCE 2 TYPE 68, QUANTITY 69-72; RESOURCE 3 TYPE 73, Q'NTY 74-76; RESOURCE 4 TYPE 77, Q'NTY 78-80.

Fig. 4.3 Activity and resource list—punched card instructions

I	J	D	DESCRIPTION	RESOURCES
190 21	22	2	SDO REVI *Proj.Report* EW/AMENDS./APPROVAL	
370(a)24	29	2	1ST,2WEE KS EMP./FREIGHT SUR.	✓ 1✓ 2
500 22	32	6	PREPARE RCAD NET. 1967/1986	✓ 1✓ 1
450(a)22	31	2	1ST,2WEE KS CAR PARKING STUDY	✓ 1✓ 1
270 24	35	2	EDIT PRO GRAM - CORDON SURVEY	✓ 1
330(a)24	28	1	1ST, WEE K HOME INT. STUDY	✓ 2
290(a)24	37	1	1ST, WEE K PUB.TRANS. SURVEY	✓ 2
670 33	67	20	DEV.MODE L PROGRAM(INC EVAL)	✓ 1
250 24(a)	26	1	1ST, WEE K OF CORDON SURVEYS	✓ 4
370(b)29	30	1	3RD,WEEK EMP./FRT. SUR.(INT)	✓ 4
460 31	49	15	CODE CAR PARK STUDY	✓ 1
450(b)31	48	14	REMAINDE R CAR PARKING STUDY	✓ 1✓ 1
340 28	45	13	CODING O F HOME INT. STUDY	✓ 2
310 33	56	2	EDIT PRO GRAM=PUB.TRANS. SUR.	✓ 1
330(b)28	44	12	LAST 12 WEEKS-HOME INT.STUDY	✓ 2
300 27	43	10	CODING P UB.TRANS. SURVEYS	✓ 2
260 26	41	9	CODING C ORDON SURVEYS	✓ 4
290(b)27	42	9	LAST 9 W EEKS PUB.TRANS. SUR.	✓ 2
250(b)26	40	8	LAST 8 W EEKS CORDON SURVEYS	✓ 4
380 30	47	12	CODING O F EMP./FRT. SURVEY	✓ 4
370(c)30	46	11	LAST 11W EEKS EMP./FRT. SUR.	✓ 4
350 30	37	2	EDIT PRO GRAM-HOME INT. STUDY	✓ 1
560 32	52	6	PREPARE PUB.TR.NET.1967/1986	✓ 1✓ 1
510 30	50	10	CONDUCT/ ~~CODE~~ TRAVEL TIME SUR	✓ 1✓ 1

Fig. 4.4   Computer output—bar chart

```
        1          10          20          30          40          50        60

        S          I           I           I           I           I         I

  •     I          I         ( X          I           I           I         I
  •     I          I         ( KK         I           I           I         I
                                  1967        1967
  1     I          I          X••••XF                 I           I         I
  2     I          I          XX,F                     I           I         I
  5     I          I          XX••••                  I           I         I
  6     I          I         X•••••                   I           I         I
  9     I          I         X•••••••F                I           I         I
  9     I          I        •I X•••••••••••••••••X,•••••••••F      I         I
                                    15
  0     I          I         •••X••••F                I           I         I
  •     I          I          K                       I           I         I
  2     I          I          X••••••••••••••X,F      I           I         I
  4     I          I          X••••••••••••X•••F      I           I         I
  5     I          I          X••••••••••••X••••F     I           I         I
  5     I          I          XX••,••F    NA          I           I         I
  5     I          I          X••••••••••X,••••F      I           I         I
  5     I          I          X••••••••••X•••••F      I           I         I
  9     I          I          X••••••••••I•••••••F    I           I         I
  9     I          I          X••••••••••I•••••••F    I           I         I
  •     I          I          X••••••••••I•••••••F    I           I         I
        I          I          KCCCCCCCCCCCCK          I           I         I
                                       95
        I          I          X••••••••••XF           I           I         I
        I          I          XX•••,•F                I           I         I
                                  1967
        I          I          X•••••XF                I           I         I
        I          I          X•••••I•••••X,,F        I           I         I
```

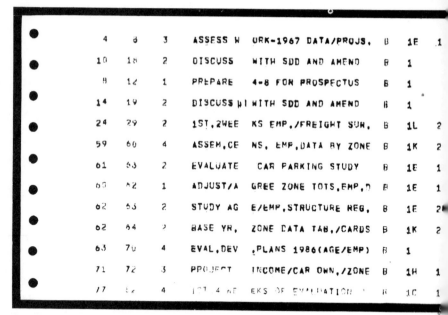

Fig. 4.5 Computer output—bar chart

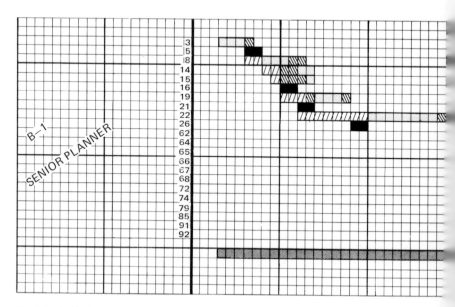

Fig. 4.6 Individual staff bar chart

```
4   I        X•X...F      I            I            I            I            I              M
4   I        X•...,F      I            I            I            I            I              ■
4   I        X•..,F       I            I            I            I            I
•   I        I   KK       I            I            I            I            I
•   I        I            KK           I            I            I            I
•   I        I            I            I            KCCK         I            I
2   I        I            I            I            IXX,F        I            I              B
•   I        I            I            I            I K          I            I              ■
•   I        I            I            I            I   KK       I            I
3   I        I            I            I            I    XX,,F   I            I
•   I        I            I            I            I    KCCK    I            I
4   I        I            I            I            I            IX•XF        I
•   I        I            I            I            I            I            K              ■
•   I        I            I            I            I            I            I
```

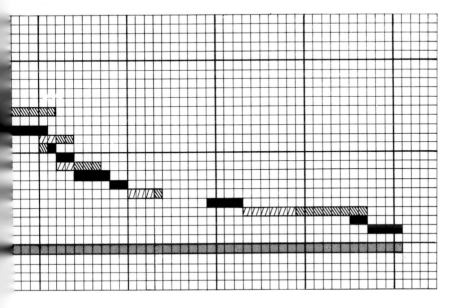

4.05 Balancing the budget

This process of adjustment led on to the next stage which formed a vital link between resource planning and cost forecasting. This was to interpret from the amended activity timings the total forecast demand for each key staff category including professional, clerical and temporary staff. Balanced staffing forecasts could thus be obtained, which could in turn be costed.

At this stage there were two alternative methods of budgetary planning available to the project manager:

1 He could cost each activity in turn whilst levelling and obtain a total planned cost. If this exceeded the budget when all direct and indirect costs were considered he could cut back pro rata across activities (in order to maintain a planned profit margin) or he could make individual adjustments

2 He could work towards pre-determined levels in certain resources within a global budget in which the cost of resource groups was allocated from the earlier estimates obtained from the network shown in Fig. 4.2.

This second method was in fact adopted, but it did have disadvantages in reducing the flexibility of resource planning when it came to decisions about relative amounts of one resource or another. This was particularly true where certain resources were used in common, that is on different activities at the same time, and it meant that arbitrary decisions were sometimes made when planning the use of skilled professional manpower. The use of the second method in this project did, however, lead to a sound project budget. In later projects the first approach was adopted and this is explained in our earlier book.

The process then carried out can best be described as cost 'levelling' and this involved consideration of resource requirements, levels and techniques and all associated costs. In effect, a cumulative statement of all these individual costs was obtained so that they could be related to the total budget sum. Adjustments could then be made to balance the totals within acceptable limits.

PROJECT *L.U.T.S.E.C.S.*   ALLOCATION No.   623 / 270

Activity number: 24, 35
Description: *Produce Edit programs for cordon/screen*
               line tabulations.

Network estimates:

D	RESOURCE ESTIMATES	SCHEDULE *13 June*
2	*H-1*	

ACTUAL PROGRESS   ++++++++++++++++xx●●●●●F++++++++++++++++

BUDGET CALCULATION:

1 Direct staff costs	2×140	280	
2 Proportion of general costs	*gen div.*	69	
		349	349
3 Estimated computer costs			30
4 Maps, printing, documents, etc			
5 Travelling			
6 Proportion of contingencies			35
Timing:		Budget figure	414

June (all)

Actual cost calculation:

MONTH	TECHN'L STAFF	SP. CLERICAL STAFF	FIELD STAFF	COMPUTER	MAPS ETC	TRAVEL EXPENSE	MONTH TOTAL	RUNNING TOTAL
March	29	—	—	—	—	—	29	29
April	112	—	—	41	—	—	153	182
May	77	—	—	26	—	—	77	285
June	17	—	—	55	—	—	72	357
July	34	—	—	—	—	—	34	391

Remarks: *Item was more "spread" than budget*
           allowed for, but was completed almost on
           schedule and within budget.

Fig. 4.7   Example of actual cost recording on activity cost

4.06 Activity costing–component costs

The activity as a coherent item of work had to be examined in detail, and for this purpose an activity costing sheet was developed. An example of this is reproduced in Fig. 4.7.

Fig. 4.7 shows four basic components of cost which had to be calculated for each activity:

1 direct staff costs
2 other direct costs
3 overhead costs including management
4 contingency allowance.

The reason for including the contingency item has been explained earlier. In a budgetary sense, it can be viewed as the means by which uncertainty can be covered. The overhead items need careful consideration and a decision had to be made on the percentage of the total budget which had to be set aside to meet reimbursable management, overhead and head office costs.

As has been explained elsewhere, the remuneration of consultants for this type of work is at hourly rates based upon the salaries of the professional staff involved. The Association of Consulting Engineers which lays down the scales of charges assumes that all office overheads and the profit margin are covered by the rates charged. Thus the use of ACE rates in calculating the budget for each item allowed us to work on 'sale value' and got over the complicated problem of allocating overhead charges as between the head office and the project office which was, in effect, a branch. In other forms of project activity in different organisations this problem has to be resolved.

Even with the great simplification of the use of ACE rates for costing, however, a way had still to be found for accounting for the technical direction of the study by the project manager whose time would not be normally allocated specifically to activities but rather to 'general direction' and there were some other costs in a similar category. These could be thought of as reimbursable overheads and in order to have a satisfactory basis both for the cost estimate and for the control of costs, such overheads were apportioned to activities pro rata to the direct costs allocated to them. A similar approach was adopted when dealing with certain key individuals' bar charts. Where, after manual resource scheduling to eliminate overloads (by using float) there appeared to be gaps in requirement for a particular resource, but the gaps were not wide enough for it to be expedient for that individual to be taken off the project for short periods, the cost was treated as a chargeable overhead for estimating purposes and spread pro rata among the other planned activities in which that individual was to be involved.

It can be seen that the production of an activity-based budget is a multi-staged process of preparing or completing the following:

1 preliminary estimates
2 an outline network
3 basic resource calculations
4 a refined network
5 detailed resource estimates
6 schedules of levelled resources
7 calculation of resource requirements by duration
8 calculations of final budget sums for each resource
9 a statement showing the apportionment of chargeable overheads into direct activities
10 the completion of activity cost forecasting forms
11 balancing the budget.

It should be explained that this perhaps somewhat complicated approach was associated with the process of appreciating the problems of the study, isolating the more difficult parts and striking a balance between economy and technical progress. In retrospect the method was very satisfactory as it led to a carefully detailed set of cost forecast allocations which in practice did give a measure of control which enabled the project to be completed in time and within the budget.

Through the steps described above the project manager planned the budget for each activity, completing the forecast for a full set of activity cost sheets. The total of these was now, by definition, his total budget and the totals from each sheet were transferred onto a summary sheet which was designed as a monthly management report.

4.07 Day-to-day control

It should be emphasised that the project network and cost control system was intended to provide an overall framework for the project. Day-to-day control was achieved, particularly during the complex survey operations when over a hundred people were involved, by the use of sub-networks, generally arranged in ladder form to show the required effort from each individual or group. The project manager found it a useful training exercise to persuade the leader of each group to draw up his own sub-network, and in this way the seeds were sown for the wider application of network planning in subsequent projects.

4.08 Management control

Considerable thought was given to the frequency of progress review and management reporting. It was decided that a monthly system should be operated. In order that this should be done it was necessary to determine the 'spend pattern' for the planned duration of each activity. Initially the newly determined duration was transferred from individual bar chart format, after re-phasing and levelling, to each activity cost sheet.

The cost sheet was designed to illustrate the agreed schedule as shown in Fig. 4.7. A forecast of the likely spend rate was then calculated. This, however, was used for comparative purposes and was not expected to become a fixed measure of later performance. The means of measuring performance which was developed will be explained later. From this spend rate data it was possible to transfer all budget data to a monthly report form of the type shown in Figs. 1.3 and 3.4.

This report was to act as the basis for management control throughout the project.

4.09 Monitoring progress

As far as possible the original planned budget in the network was left unchanged throughout the project. This was only possible whilst the planned basis for operation remained acceptable as a whole. Minor variations were not allowed to upset the overall plan but were accepted as normal within the system.

Having created a detailed budget it was now necessary to ensure that actual costs were recorded and collated *on the same activity basis as planned costs*. Special efforts were made to ensure that all staff costs, both local and head office, all transactions and all reimbursable overhead costs were brought into one common administrative sieve. This, by its nature, cut across the requirements for normal accounting but it did not replace them.

All staff had to be made familiar with the project plan and its associated cost numbers. They were required to complete monthly time sheets. It was already common practice to do this and the resulting returns were already used as the basis for invoicing clients. The extra step now necessary was to state which activities within the project had been worked on and for how many hours each month, quoting the relevant cost numbers.

Similarly for transactions and reimbursable overhead costs a screening process was necessary to ensure that all costs attributable to the study were properly allocated to activities and were verified by the project manager as fair charges to the project. In the early stages of the project it was found difficult to eliminate errors and delay caused by the by-passing of the new system in such matters as invoices from suppliers which tended to lag somewhat in time from the point when the cost was actually incurred. It was decided that the whole system should be based upon costs as they were incurred and not on bills as they were paid. Thus a rigid system had to be enforced to ensure that all such paper work was received by the project manager for verification as early as possible. In order to eliminate the problem of time lag between carrying out work and recording its cost all expenses were coded to activities on a committed basis prior to payment and actual monthly costs were collated by activity to enable direct comparison to be made between costs and the forecasts contained in the activity budgets.

For purposes of management reporting and comparison with the budget all costs were calculated manually on the "sales value" basis (i.e. at ACE rate). All the budget totals in the activity cost sheets and the management reports were stated in these terms.

In effect this meant that the report did not give a direct indication of profit in money terms. It was not designed to do this. What it did achieve was a measure of direct comparison between planned cost and actual cost in terms of the effort which had been expended and of the money and man-hours budgeted as available for each particular activity. Provided actual performance matched the original estimate, costs were covered and profit was achieved.

4.10 Central administration

Although this particular project was the prototype within the firm, and most of the costing calculations were performed by hand in the project office, the head office administration was fast developing a new computer program to process all monthly costs for manpower, materials and other operating expenses. The basis for this program has been described in Chapter Two. It took a considerable time before it became accurate enough to replace manual calculations carried out in the project office.

In order to reach the required degree of accuracy, where the print-out for all the firm's projects could be accepted for management control on the one hand and for invoicing clients on the other, it was necessary to ensure close control over the data returned monthly to head office. This included monthly time sheets for all personnel with specific instructions relating to invoicing, together with verified, cost-allocated invoices and statements of expenses. Coding could then be commenced by the accounts staff. The input to the program consisted of the man hours for each staff member on each activity worked on, identified by staff category (for charging purposes), and a list of all transactions and expenses incurred. Of the latter, it was necessary to identify those which were reimbursable at cost, in which case entries were shown in input columns for credit as well as debit.

Resulting statements were produced with the computed actual cost and sale values shown for each activity and for the project as a whole. Fig. 4.8 shows the format of the output although, naturally, it is necessary to delete actual costs and names in a document of this nature.

The statement has an attractive clarity. It summarises all staff costs for the month by staff category and a clear indication of profitability can be obtained by comparing debit and credit columns.

4.11 The conduct of the project and progress review

Progress was measured by the calculation at the end of each month of the value of work done for each activity. Value was defined for this purpose as the percentage of the activity completed multiplied by the activity budget. Fig. 4.9 gives an example.

The relevant columns to consider are the "total budget" and "% complete". The product of these gives the "value of work done" figures. It should be remembered that these figures were calculated in ACE rate terms. The important comparison was therefore between the amount spent in ACE terms on each activity and the value of work done. The accuracy of the calculation depended, of course, upon the project manager's own estimate of the percentage completion of each item which is an important point to consider when deciding on the number of activities to include in a project network. The smaller the item the easier it is to calculate its state of completion.

This systematic assessment at the end of each month allowed the project manager to consider the significance of variations and to be able to forecast any likely overspending. This could then either be brought under control or, alternatively, raised with the client to decide whether it could be warranted for some particular technical or other reason. Adjustments could then be made to the budget or the programme and decisions could be reached on how to achieve balancing economies.

In this particular project it was found, as had been expected, that overspending and underspending on individual items were roughly in balance except in the case of one large and important item where it turned out that a considerable under-estimate had occurred in the planning stage. The activity had been phased to run over a period of four months and the cost control system made the probability of overspending apparent after only two months. This warning was given in sufficient time for the project manager to make a drastic revision to the manpower and effort which had been planned for another activity, while at the same time he applied stringent economy to the remainder of the offending activity. This particular example, perhaps more than any other single aspect of the entire system advocated by our book, convinced us of its value.

```
PROJECT NUMBER    990 SUFFIX   154

GRANGEMTH FALKIRK A R S

PROJECT BEGAN MONTH 10 YEAR 71
PROJECT IS RUN FROM OFFICE  8 OF COMPANY
CHARGING  PROCEDURE 0


                                              PERSON

MONTH              STAFF         STAFF NAME
                   GRADE


      11             0            CAMERON MI
      11             0            MCCAIG E
      11             0            STARES S,
      11             0            STARES S,

                                    TOTAL F
      11             1            GAULD,MRS
      11             1            JONES MRS.

                                    TOTAL F


              TOTAL FOR PERSONNEL COSTS AND



MONTH              ITEM          DESCRIPTION


      11            1030          EDIN XEROX C
      11            1040          EDIN EXPS EC
      11            1040          EDIN EXPS EC
      11            1040          EDIN EXPS EC
      11            1040          EDIN EXPS EC
      11            1040          V131-11 LIME




                                 ACCUMULATIVE TO

                                 ACCUMULAT
```

Fig. 4.8   Monthly report sheet format—computer print out

COST ACCOUNTS NOVEMBER 1971

PROJECT DIRECTOR ████████

STS AND CHARGES

HOURS	DIRECT COSTS	FEE AT ACE RATES
2.0	████	████
7.0	███	███
92.0	█████	█████
3.0	████	████
DE 104.0	█████	█████
18.0	████	████
1.5	██	
DE 19.5	███	███
S 123.5	████	████

SACTIONS

	DEBIT	CREDIT
J	1,570	1,570
ARES	28,940	28,940
TARES	15,420	15,420
TARES	3,250	3,250
TARES	2,730	2,730
HOTEL	17,500	17,500
FOR TRANSACTIONS	69,410	69,410
AL FOR JOB/SUFFIX	████	████
EGINNING OF MONTH	████	████
L AT END OF MONTH	████	████

5 Examples of use in the construction industry

5.01 Introduction

One of the authors, Peter McIlroy, was intimately concerned from 1957 to 1959 with the construction of the framework of a very large building which forms part of the power station at Aberthaw in South Wales. We think that this operation can be used to provide an example of the way in which network planning and cost control can be applied in the construction industry. It must be understood that the techniques which are now described were not available at that time and this Chapter takes the opportunity to compare the way in which the project was actually managed with the way in which the authors would tackle it today.

The reader may think that this particular example is rather specialised and may even find it difficult to follow all the twists and turns in the description of how the building frame was put up. We think, however, that almost any other example from life in the construction industry would have been as complicated; and we hope that some of the sense of deep involvement with, and enthusiasm for the project, which seems to be a characteristic of engineers working with large and potentially dangerous structures, will be communicated in our descriptions.

5.02 General description of the project

Fig. 5.1 gives some idea of the scale of the building. It shows the structural steelwork frame of the main part of the power station—the boiler house—and the concrete columns and beams which framed the separate but adjoining turbine house. The

76

Fig. 5.1   Turbine House frame at Aberthaw Power Station—guyed derrick in
position for column erection

picture also shows the size of the enormous crane which had to
be used for the erection of the turbine house frame.

The framework consisted of columns about 70 feet long
weighing 56 tons; main roof beams about 120 feet long
weighing 51 tons each; edge and fascia beams generally about
40 feet long; and 40 feet crane-beams which had to be set in
line on ledges or corbels on the inside faces of the columns
about two-thirds of the way up. The roof itself was composed
of precast concrete units spanning between the main roof
beams.

The function of the building is to keep the weather out of the area where six huge generators operate and to provide support for a gantry crane which can move up and down the turbine house over the generators to lift sections of the machines during installation and maintenance. In most earlier Power Stations the turbine house frame had been built in structural steelwork but the design engineers had decided that in this instance they would use prestressed concrete. This presented the designers and the contractors with a whole range of new problems, some of which are described later in this Chapter, not so much for their technical interest but for the management difficulties which they created.

5.03 Control structure for the project

This project was typical of the way in which civil engineering and building in Britain is organised, and many other countries use the same method. The client—in this case the Central Electricity Authority which was later reconstituted as the Central Electricity Generating Board—employed a firm of specialist consulting engineers to take on overall responsibility for the design of the power station to their general specification. These consultants, Merz and McLellan, were concerned with the mechanical and electrical design and the way in which they wanted the power station to work when it was complete. Rendel, Palmer and Tritton were commissioned as consulting civil engineers to design the buildings and foundations for the power station, the access arrangements for road vehicles and coal, and the culverts to bring sea water in through the turbines and then to discharge the hot water back into the sea.

The two firms of consulting engineers arranged for competitive tenders from contractors for the various parts of the work on the site. John Morgan (Builders) Ltd. were appointed as the main contractor. They were responsible for building the turbine house frame which we are using for our example, as well as many other things at Aberthaw. They, in turn, employed two specialist sub-contractors: Dowmac (Products) Ltd., who were experts in the manufacture of precast concrete units; and Costain John Brown Ltd., who were specialists in the design and operation of very large cranes.

Fig. 5.2 illustrates the relationships between the various firms directly involved in the erection of the turbine house frame.

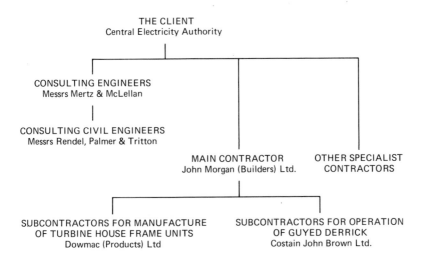

THE CLIENT
Central Electricity Authority

CONSULTING ENGINEERS
Messrs Mertz & McLellan

CONSULTING CIVIL ENGINEERS
Messrs Rendel, Palmer & Tritton

MAIN CONTRACTOR
John Morgan (Builders) Ltd.

OTHER SPECIALIST
CONTRACTORS

SUBCONTRACTORS FOR MANUFACTURE
OF TURBINE HOUSE FRAME UNITS
Dowmac (Products) Ltd

SUBCONTRACTORS FOR OPERATION
OF GUYED DERRICK
Costain John Brown Ltd.

Fig. 5.2   Firms involved in the Turbine House frame erection at Aberthaw

Fig. 5.3 shows, side by side, the lines of responsibility among the staff of the consulting civil engineers and the main contractor.

Fig. 5.3 probably needs more explanation in order to make clear where the responsibilities lay. The consulting engineer's design office in London was responsible for the design of the turbine house frame. The main contractor was responsible for all the arrangements for manufacturing and erecting the frame, the site engineer/agent Mr. S. A. Vincent being given the day-to-day responsibility for this. Peter McIlroy was his section engineer for the frame and had the job of planning the operation in detail including technical responsibility for the quality of materials and workmanship. Direct control of site personnel was, as always, the responsibility of the general foreman and the specialist trade foremen and gangers, but on any particular project, especially a difficult one like this, a very close relationship evolves between the section foreman and his men and the section engineer, who between them form the team for the project.

The engineer's representative on site had the responsibility of seeing that the designs were carried out properly and therefore 'matched' the contractor's site staff with section engineers and site inspectors.

Fig. 5.3 does not show the specialist sub-contractors. These both owed allegiance to the main contractor and, in both cases, it was essential that their timetables and preparatory work

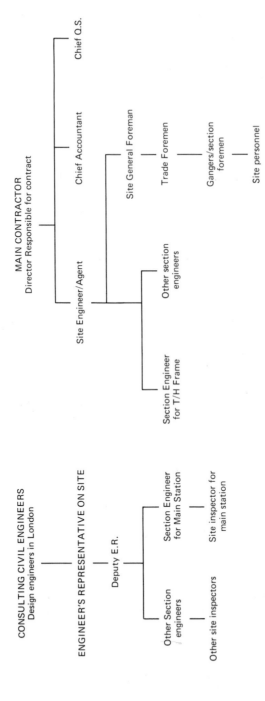

Fig. 5.3 Relationships between consulting engineers and contractors—Aberthaw Power Station

should be linked in with the main programme of work. In each case design staff were involved in the sub-contractor's head office, and site staff controlled their own operations on site.

5.04 Cost control

Generally in civil engineering contracts the design engineers measure the amount of each type of material, such as concrete or earth to be excavated and moved, and these are set out in the form of a Bill of Quantities. The contractor estimates how much each cubic yard of concrete is going to cost to produce and put in place and sets this rate against the quantity in the Bill. Multiplying the quantity by the rate gives the estimated cost for all the concrete in that item. The contractor is held to that rate even if, on final measurement, the quantity is found to be different from the original estimate. However, if the contractor is able to prove that circumstances beyond his control made it more expensive to place each cubic yard of concrete, he can make a claim for additional payment. The consulting engineer advises the client on whether or not such a claim is justified and occasionally the contractor's claims are pushed to the point of arbitration if agreement cannot be reached.

Thus, in a case like the turbine house frame, the contractor must get a complete understanding of the requirements of the design, which are generally given in a written specification, and must work out in some detail how he is going to carry out the job before making his estimates which will form the basis of his eventual payment. This task is normally the responsibility of the Quantity Surveyor, but in a complicated case the work has to be planned in better-than-average detail and the section engineer is probably in the best position to do this. Once the contract is under way, the contractor and the consulting engineer agree each month on the quantity of each item which has been completed during the month and the contractor then submits an interim account for payment. This is generally paid after checking but a proportion of the account is retained as a form of guarantee against the results of poor workmanship coming out at a later stage.

5.05 The use of a network and cost control system

In 1957 network planning was still in its infancy and the

technique was not available. The project was planned using bar charts and a strip-cartoon illustrative technique to give as clear as possible a picture of each step in the sequence. In addition, it quickly became clear that the arrangement of lifting tackle was going to be a critical feature of the project so that a scale model was built to give everyone concerned a vivid picture of what they would be up against.

Thus, while we are now convinced that a network planning technique would have been the ideal way of organising and controlling this project, we are not in any sense implying criticism of the way in which the work was actually done; far from it, as Peter McIlroy, who was in the thick of it, looks back on this as the exercise in project planning which really taught him to begin thinking in embryo networks and allowed him to recognise the value of network planning when he was first introduced to it formally five or six years later.

What should a network and cost control system set out to achieve in a project like this?

(i) General appreciation

The management should be able to get a good general appreciation of the timetable, the major problems, and the way in which the manufacturing schedule and production of lifting equipment should be tied in with the overall programme. For this reason management also requires at the earliest stage of planning a careful analysis of the requirements of the design so as to get a reliable estimate of the length of time needed for each cycle in the erection process.

(ii) Communication

All parties to the project need to have an easily-understood picture of the way in which things fit in to one another. In this case the design incorporated many new features and the contractors needed to make sure they had appreciated all their implications. For instance, they had to decide to what extent the timing of the erection of one unit depended on the tensioning of certain prestressing wires in another, which in turn had to wait until the concrete in a particular joint in the frame had reached a certain age and strength. In addition, each firm needs to have before it a clear 'statement' of the project which would allow it to assess the implications of delay in any part of the preparatory work, in order to decide whether a modification to the design of a particular element would have a delaying effect on the erection sequence or on the cost of production.

(iii) Delegation

The management of each firm needs a means for deciding which parts of their own responsibilities could be delegated, the main contractor to his sub-contractors, the design engineer to his representative on site, the site agent for the contractor to his section engineer.

(iv) Meeting deadlines

It is necessary to have a method of isolating deadlines for critical items. Aberthaw provided many:

- (a) Dowmac (Products) Ltd. needed to know the full details of stainless steel "bend anchors" to be cast into the columns and beams during manufacture of the big units, in time to be able to order the special steel from the manufacturers and in time for the bend anchors to be tested and delivered.
- (b) The main contractor needed to work out the date for completion of the pit which had to be made on site to house the units during their manufacture (see Fig. 5.4), so as to plan the construction of the pit and to coordinate the delivery by Dowmac of the special equipment to be built in.
- (c) All concerned needed to have a programme worked out in such a way that the first turbine could be delivered and placed by a certain date followed at intervals by the remaining five turbines.

(v) Control of operations

Everyone needs a comprehensive plan for the project which can be used as a method for recording progress and assessing the implications of lateness in any one aspect of the work. This was a classic example of a case in which four quite separate sets of management needed a plan which would allow them to control their own activities to fit in with the common objective.

Fig. 5.4   Pits built for the manufacture of columns and beams at Aberthaw

(vi) Planning and controlling for profit

Contractors are in business to make a profit. Each management concerned in this project needed to be able to organise his own work as efficiently as possible within a common framework so as to be able to make as much profit as possible and at the same time avoid the risk of being held liable, in very real financial terms, for extra costs incurred by the others owing to his own failure to produce on time.

A well constructed network linked with a cost control system could provide for all these requirements. The remainder of this chapter describes how, had the authors been placed today in the position occupied by Peter McIlroy in 1957, they would go through the various steps in the management process, creating a project plan for exercising operational control over the activities of the main contractor and his sub-contractors and setting up a project budget for the achievement of internal control and profitability.

5.06 Significant features in the construction schedule

While this chapter is not really concerned with anything but the erection of the frame, the planning of the erection is clearly linked with the rate at which the units can be constructed, tested and delivered to the point of erection. Thus one starting point for the planning of the construction schedule must be to establish when the units are needed and then to check that it is possible to produce them in time.

The sheer size and weight of the units is, of course, in itself a significant feature. With the lives of men at stake, every single step in the process of making and putting up these units must be thought out and tested in some way to make sure that nothing has been overlooked and nothing unsafe is being done. This means that a generous allowance must be made in the plan for the first time each operation is to be carried out, giving a chance for all three teams (the makers of the units, the operators of the guyed derrick and ourselves) to learn by experience the easiest and safest way to work.

Prestressing of concrete is nowadays quite commonplace and many elegant structures depend upon this for their strength. The stressing of the concrete in the turbine house frame was considered in 1957 to be quite advanced and required non-standard equipment; so that the schedule had to allow a reasonable time for stressing methods to be learned on the site.

Fig. 5.5 shows in a very simplified manner what is meant by prestressing concrete. The upper diagram shows a concrete beam spanning between two supports and shows that the beam tends to sag under its own weight and that of any load imposed on it, creating tension in the concrete near the bottom of the beam and compression in the concrete near the top of it. The lower diagram shows how, by applying pressure to the two ends of the beam, one introduces contrary stresses in the concrete which counteract the effect of the beam's own weight and allow more weight to be added to the top of the beam without placing intolerable stress on the concrete which is strong in compression but not in tension. The squeeze on the ends of the

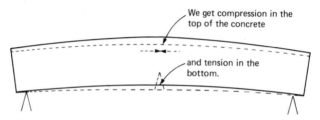

We get compression in the top of the concrete

and tension in the bottom.

a) Beam tends to sag under its own weight and any loads imposed on it.

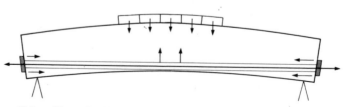

b) By pulling a wire tight and holding it we put forces into the beam which relieve the "sag" and allow us to add more weight.

Fig. 5.5   Simplified explanation of prestressing concrete

beams is applied by pulling the two ends of a wire or steel bar, using hydraulic jacks, anchoring the wire or bar when the required amount of stress has been applied.

Three different methods of applying prestress were used at Aberthaw in the turbine house. For the first, the column and beam units were stressed during manufacture in the pits illustrated in Fig. 5.4 by pulling the wires tight and casting the concrete around them, subsequently cutting the ends of the wires and allowing the tension in them to be transferred into compression in the concrete. For the second and third methods, hollow tubes were cast into the concrete in the pits. The stress was then applied to the units during and after the erection of the frame by passing either cables or steel bars through the hollow tubes and pulling from each end. The design engineers had calculated how much stress needed to be applied at each stage in the erection of the frame and had specified that, as the loads were applied gradually (for example, as the roof was placed on to the roof beams) so the post-tensioning should be gradually increased to counteract the effect of the added weights.

It can be seen then that the erection sequence and the length of time and cost involved are very much dependent on the success of the prestressing. This, in turn, depends upon the concrete in the joints in the frame achieving maturity as quickly as possible. All these factors must be taken into account in planning the erection sequence.

5.07 Estimating the erection cycle time

Because of the complexities of the design requirements a "landscape" type of project network cannot, in this instance, be completed without taking a very close look at the implications of these problems. Thus the first step is to work out a detailed network of everything that has to happen until an operating cycle can be established. Once this is done it can be fitted in to an overall project network.

The method of creating the network as usual is quite straightforward. Activities are listed with notes on their possible duration and their dependence on other activities. Four groups of activity are isolated, those concerned with the actual erection process, those concerned with creating access to the frames by scaffolding, those concerned in placing concrete in the joints of the frame, and finally those concerned with stressing the post-tensioning cables and bars.

Although the reader need not wade through the whole list of activities, this is given in full in Fig. 5.6 to give as clear as possible a picture of the reasons behind the sequence which emerges in the network which is shown in Fig. 5.7

The network takes the process as far as is necessary to establish the operating cycle for the rest of the building and also provides the key supply dates.

5.08 Estimating complete project duration and cost

The creation of the first network (Fig. 5.7) allows the contractor and sub-contractors to get together, to discuss the erection in detail and to coordinate their efforts to fit supply to demand. It also allows decisions to be made on such things as the desirability of working continuously seven days a week, allowing gangs to take staggered but regular breaks without holding up the progress of the frame. Apart from this, some estimate has to be made of the effect of bad weather before agreeing on a cycle time to be used in the overall schedule. Once this is done, however, the creation of the overall network is a relatively simple matter, the only other detailed problem requiring special attention being the way in which the last two or three frames are put together and the guyed derrick is

Activity No.	DESCRIPTION	Estd. Durn.	DEPENDENCY
		days	erection & testing of derrick
1-2	Erect column A1	3	supply and testing of col.
2-3	Erect column B1	3	supply and testing of col.
3-4	Erect roof beam 1	3	supply and testing of beam
10-11	Scaffolding for access to frame 1—part	2	start after event 2.
11-12	Ditto—complete across beam	3	start after event 4.
4-5	Deliver beams bay 1-2, stack.	2	4.
5-6	Move derrick to serve bay 1-2	4	5.
16-17	Concrete toes of cols A1 and B1	1	start after 12.
22-23	Concrete joints between cols & beam 1	1	start after 12.
17-18	Allow concrete to mature to 6000lb/sq.in	7	follow 17 and 23.
23-24	Ditto.	7	
28-29	Stress $\frac{1}{3}$ of post-tension wires in cols and beam on frame 1	5	follows 18 and 24.
6-7	Erect column A2	3	
7-8	Erect column B2	3	
8-9	Erect beam 2.	1	
13-14	Scaffolding for access to frame 2—part	4	start after 7
14-15	Ditto—complete across beam	2	start after 9
19-20	Concrete toes of columns A2 and B2	1	
25-26	Concrete joints between cols & beam 2	1	
20-21	Allow concrete to mature to 6000lb/sq.in	7	after 20 and 26
26-27			
30-31	Stress bars at foot of col B2	1	after 21
32-33	Stress $\frac{1}{3}$ of post-tension wires in cols and beam on frame 2	3	follows 21 and 27
34-35	Erect four beams in bay 1-2 and secure to columns	2	follows 33 and 29
35-36	Erect 11 roof units in bay 1-2	2	follows 35
37-38	Stress second $\frac{1}{3}$ of wires in frames 1 & 2	4	follows 36
39-40	Erect 18 more roof units in bay 1-2	2	
40-41	Move derrick to serve bay 2-3	2	
41-42	Deliver four beams bay 2-3, stack.	2	
42-43	Erect column A3	2	
43-44	Erect column B3	2	
44-45	Erect beam 3	1	
46-47	Scaffolding for access to frame 3—start	3	follows 43
47-48	Ditto—complete across beam	2	follows 45
49-50	Concrete toes of cols A3 and B3	1	follows 48

Fig. 5.6   Turbine House erection—activity list—sheets 1 and 2

Activity No.	DESCRIPTION	Estd. Durn.	DEPENDENCY
52-53	Concrete joints between cols & beam 3	1	follows 48
50-51	} Allow concrete to mature to 6000lb/sq.in	7	follows 50 and 53
53-54	}		
55-56	Stress bars at toe of col B3	1	follows 51
57-58	Stress $\frac{1}{3}$ wires in frame 3	2	follows 56
59-60	Erect four beams in bay 2-3	2	follows 58
60-61	Erect 11 roof units in bay 2-3	2	follows 60
62-63	Stress crane beams on cols A2, B2	2	follows 60
64-65	Concrete crane beam joints with columns A1, B1, A2 and B2	1	follows 63
65-76	Allow concrete to mature to 6000lb/sq.in	7	
66-67	Stress second $\frac{1}{3}$ wires in frame 3	2	follows 61
68-69	Erect 18 roof units in bay 2-3	2	follows 67
69-70	Move guyed derrick to serve bay 3-4	2	
70-71	Deliver beams for bay 3-4	2	
71-72	Erect column A4	2	
72-73	Erect column B4	2	
73-74	Erect beam 4	1	
77-78	Stress crane beams to cols, lines 1 & 2	1	follows 76
79-80	Stress final $\frac{1}{3}$ wires in frames 1 & 2	3	follows 78
81-82	Infill concrete in crane & edge beams in bay 1-2	1	follows 80
74-75	Erect final roof units in bay 1-2	1	follows 80
83-84	Scaffolding for access to frame 4—part	5	follows 72

cycle established.

dismantled. Fig. 5.8 shows the overall network which can be used for project control and communication with the consulting engineers.

Cost estimating and the creation of a budget is, as pointed out in section 5.04, rather a complex matter under the normal method of measurement and payment for civil engineering contracts. We think that it would be much simpler and much better to build up the cost estimate on the basis of the network of activities required by the design and produce a budget for each activity. The existing method gives no help in measuring the progress of an awkward job like this one, except in a very general way, whereas a cost control system linked in with the network could be enormously valuable.

In this case, the network allows us to see the required output from each gang of specialists. We can gauge whether some of them need to be treated as continuous costs to the turbine house and which of them can be phased in with other work elsewhere in the power station, and this enables us to estimate cost with reasonable accuracy and to allocate these in a sensible fashion to each activity.

It is scarcely necessary to illustrate this in full detail. It should be obvious that almost all the activities depend upon manpower and, although expensive materials are used, it is surely better to base the cost estimate on knowledge of how many men are required to do each part of the job than to base it on so many pounds per cubic foot of concrete, which is the traditional method of estimating and payment.

5.09 The control system in use

Having used the first network (Fig. 5.7) to establish the operating cycle, and the second network (Fig. 5.8) to give the overall picture, day to day control is achieved by the use of sub-networks to approximately the same degree of detail as the operating cycle network. Activities are numbered systematically with two digits identifying the location of the activity. That is to say, each activity is numbered and each time it is repeated in the next cycle it is given a similar number to represent the type of activity with a two digit prefix to indicate which bay of the building it is in. It is normal for each ganger and foreman to keep a detailed record of the number of hours worked by each of his men in the form of a time sheet. By using the correct allocation numbers it is quite simple for the accounts department to collect all manpower costs related to each activity. Similarly, the use of the same allocation numbers for materials allows the picture to be completed and the accountant is then able to provide figures for the project manager at regular intervals to show how performance compares with budget.

Armed with this information, the project manager can do some or all of the following things.

(i) Profitability control

By identifying the critical path through the network he can see the extent to which extra effort in some items can produce time savings in others. In this case the most expensive item is keeping the guyed derrick waiting and obviously anything which can be done to speed up the maturing of in-situ concrete and the stressing of units is going to minimise the derrick's standing time. Thus, if the actual cost records show that cost is going above budget in the early stages then the project manager can concentrate his energy and ingenuity (that is what engineering means) on devising quicker methods of stressing or introducing night shifts for this work. The network and the cost records give him all the information he needs to decide on the most economical course of action.

(ii) Communication

We think that by now it is self evident that the network provides a magnificent method of communication. It can be used at all levels. It can show sub-contractors the consequence of lateness in supply. It can give targets and the basis for incentive payments to the various gangs of specialists and workmen involved. It can be used as an explicit and detailed progress chart.

(iii) Fair price for the job

In almost all civil engineering contracts unforeseen circumstances interfere with the smooth running of the job. If these are caused by the contractor's own activities he has to suffer the consequences, but if they are outside his control he usually has the opportunity of making a case to the consulting engineer for additional payment. This is often a very difficult and sometimes very embarrassing process, particularly when the contractor decides that his delay is because of some act or omission of the consulting engineer. We think that the use of a detailed network can help to isolate problems of this sort, putting them and keeping them in their true perspective. By tradition, contractor's claims tend to be exaggerated and consulting engineers tend to be severe in dealing with them. The use of the network and the cost control system outlined above can, if accepted by both sides, provide a reasonable way of arriving at a balanced result and a fair price.

5.10 Theory versus practice

At the beginning of the chapter we emphasised that networking and cost control systems such as this simply did not exist in 1957, so that, in making some points of comparison between what actually happened and what might have happened under a system of network planning and cost control, we are not implying any criticism of any of the parties involved.

The planning was, in fact, good on the contractor's side. As the project was so obviously complicated, much time was devoted to working out the sequence of operations. This even included making a working scale model of half the turbine house and of the guyed derrick so that everyone concerned could get a really good visual impression of the problems. The sequence shown in the network on Fig. 5.7 was drawn out like a "strip-cartoon" and all the site engineers—consultants, contractors and sub-contractors—had a good idea from this of how the frame was to be put together. However, it was very difficult to fit so many interlocking pieces into the traditional bar chart and the main problem which was encountered during the course of the project was that of communication.

There were a great many delays before any units were erected, caused at least in part by difficulties in coordinating design details with the building of the special pieces of equipment needed to manufacture the units. While we do not suggest that these could have been avoided simply by using a network, it might well have been possible to foresee these more clearly and to lessen their impact on the project.

The use of the network might also, as stated earlier, have highlighted the fact that the post-tensioning of the columns and beams was the critical factor in the time needed for the erection of the frame. This might have affected the design engineers' decisions on the exact details of the tensioning, for instance they might have used standardised pieces of equipment instead of special ones.

Without wanting to labour the point we think that the use of a traditional bill of quantities was the aspect which could most effectively have been improved by the use of networking and cost control linked to the network. No-one was able, when using the Bill of Quantities, to assess whether or not the frame was going to be built within its budget until it was far too late for anything to be done about the effect of delays. The inevitable consequence was a claim by the contractor for extra payment.

Perhaps this makes rather gloomy reading. Let us finish on a more cheerful note by saying that this remarkable structure was built without loss of life and that all of those who worked on it, the designers, the contractors and the sub-contractors look back on it with a mixture of pride and affection, in spite of the grey hairs which they all collected in the process.

Fig. 5.9   Aberthaw Power Station—erecting a column

Part three - Further developments

6 - Towards the development of a fully integrated data processing system for operational and financial control

6.01 The background

For many years the computer programs available for critical path scheduling, network planning, PERT and the various other derivatives of these techniques have been evolving from the relatively simple 'time only' programs, towards more sophisticated processing. Reference to the DOD-NASA PERT-COST SYSTEMS, developed in the United States*, will show the reader how the early thinking was concerned with the integration of network planning and accounting systems. Fig. 6.1 shows a work breakdown structure and the basic method of coding in relation to the assembly of a typical manufactured item and to accounting codes based on functional identity. The system operated on the basis of 'work packages' and was concerned with functional cost aggregation in relation to the project rather than to activity costs.

The emphasis in these early systems was on traditional accounting codes and aggregation of costs into management summaries by cost group, by organisation and by responsibility. They were not activity cost based, and suffered from certain limitations in the data processing sense as an involved manual stage was necessary between the time processing computations, (producing basic network schedules) and the resource and cost computation producing management reports.

Further development has in fact met some of these criticisms, and the ICL PERT** system, available since 1966, made a

---

* 'PERT-COST for the new DOD and NASA requirements' by David M. Stires and Raymond P. Wenig, Industrial Education Institute, Boston, Mass., U.S.A.

** ICL User Manual "Network Planning"—PERT application system—1900 Series.

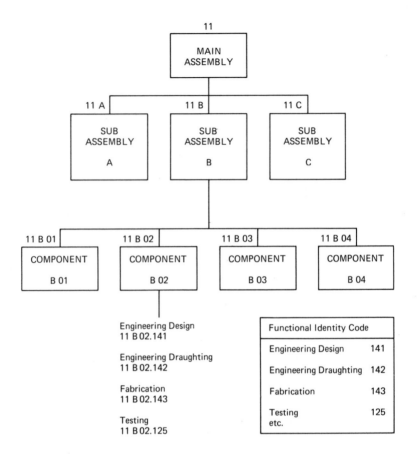

Fig. 6.1   PERT-COST project work breakdown and cost structure

significant advance. At that time ICT (now ICL) wrote in their PERT Users Manual—

"The subject of cost control is controversial and subject to many forms of application and interpretation. The facilities in the program aim essentially at providing a type of control that is directly linked with a network, and which by its nature must be considered as a method of direct costing; but special cost orientated activities (called hammocks) may be used to provide a medium for indirect cost measurement."

This was a great improvement with the essential feature that it was a direct costing technique and employed the special method of dealing with overhead costs shown in Fig. 6.2. The thinking and methodology were not, however, absolutely committed to the activity cost concept and whilst the aggrega-

tion of cost by project or sub-project was extremely useful ICL
went on to say that

"to assess the progress of a project which is under way, these
figures for the original plan must be compared with:
   2 actual value of work done to date
   3 actual cost to date
   4 revised planned cost
for the project.
All these figures may be required for the project as a whole
but they may also be calculated for sub-division of a project
which may be as small as individual activities, but which will

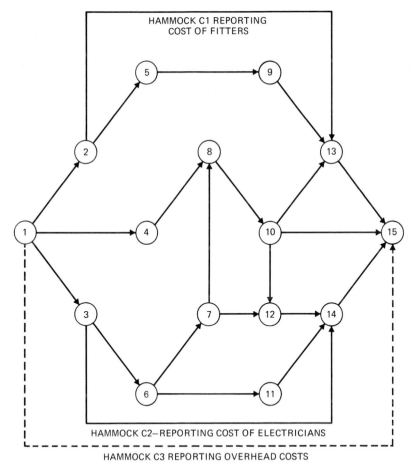

Fig. 6.2   "Hammock" activity approach to "general" costs

more usually be groups of activities divided by reference to their cost codes."*

In other words they were still more concerned with the accounting approach to budgetary planning which considered cost groupings, than with the cost associated with operations and activities as such. We firmly believe that the emphasis should be on the activity costing approach with all overhead costs allocated to activities. Our experience has shown the value of this in controlling the progress and profitability of projects. We are concerned, therefore, with the development of computer software which carries out the requirements referred to by ICL and which combines in one process the time scheduling, resource levelling, cost planning and review of progress function: preferably on a double entry basis to tie up debits and credits with relevant ledgers.

ICL's 1900 Series software in fact goes a long way towards achieving that (leaving aside the double-entry aspects), but adopts an approach on cost input which 'marries-up' with their particular method of resource input and scheduling. The computations are based on initial average costs for a resource during a time period weighted by calculated usage in that time period, with a hunt for lower average cost areas in resource scheduling, leading to a solution of 'least cost schedule'.

Then,

"the second main stage of the calculation extends the resource usage of individual activities by the average prices to obtain for each activity a planned cost. From the foregoing it is clear that the cost of any activity will depend on where it is scheduled." **

and further

"most of the above depends on the fact that different costs have been specified for the normal and threshold use of resources."

Thus the ICL approach had taken a step forward but was still subject to limitations in certain respects:

1 It averaged resource cost by time period and searched, through resource scheduling, for least cost

2 It could not work down to a cost ceiling

* PERT Users Guide—ICL—See 5.2—2nd Edition 1967

** PERT Users Guide—ICL—See 5.4—2nd Edition 1967

3 It was not wholly committed to activity costing, particularly for overhead costs, and it was recognised that

"frequently, however, the method for collection of actual costs will bear little resemblance to the structure of the network . . ." *

In other words it was a more sophisticated way of adapting to normal accounting procedures.

The Authors do not accept normal accounting procedures for purposes of project control and are convinced that an organisation which is project orientated must adapt the whole of its data processing including cost accountancy to the 'activity cost' concept.

To obtain realistic control it is necessary for most organisations to consider this approach. We do not believe that the work package approach is as meaningful in cost planning and control terms as a system totally committed in the cost forecasting, budget setting and actual cost reviewing stages, to individual activities. The main reason for holding this view is that the actual operation of a project depends upon its activities. This implies that the activity base used for costing is a coherent, measurable and recognisable entity, and that a tangible result is achieved from it.

What then are the basic requirements for an integrated operational and costing system which might avoid some of the pitfalls?

6.02 The basic criteria for an integrated program

(i) Input

To be able to receive data relating to activities on:

1 I–J
2 Duration
3 Description
4 Resources

and further to receive instructions relating to the following.

1 Basic rates and costs, for variable costs and resource data
2 The rate(s) or formula for calculating value and charge
3 The information relating to fixed costs, with the options to spend a total figure in certain proportions, for example

* PERT Users Guide–ICL–See 5.7–2nd Edition 1967

pro rata in relation to a chosen breakdown

4 The project durations (including sub-area durations) and a cost ceiling which may require cost manipulation during processing

5 The treatment of costs where demand in a time period exceeds supply. This does not necessarily imply overtime, but where this is required either a separate rate would be input or another means of treating such costs would have to be provided for

6 The areas of uncertainty where alternative ranges of resources may be specified, allowing a least cost solution to an activity to be calculated. Alternatively during processing the initial over-runs could be indicated so that instructions on where and how to cut back can be input

7 The data in respect of transactions not subject to any computations, both debit and credit, in order that the output can be directly tied up with the invoicing and ledger entry procedures

8 Penalty costs which must be added to direct costs for given delays affecting overall duration

9 The actual progress at any time of review, in terms of time, resources, costs and percentage completion

(ii) Computation

To incorporate the basic features of a PERT-type program in respect of network calculations and output, and then to—

1 Carry out resource levelling calculations

2 Calculate basic costs for each activity and for the project

3 Adjust according to operators instructions the resource usage patterns where necessary to achieve a balanced budget and resource plan, isolating 'areas' of overload/ overtime for review. The operator should have the facility to make adjustments to rates, or resource forecasts for this purpose.

4 Calculate the spread of overheads in accordance with instructions on initial input, or latterly from the operator, in accordance with a flexible formula for allocation.

5 Calculate from the basic rates and resources the activity costs, working in terms of rates relating to a chosen time base: i.e. hourly, half-daily, daily or weekly. The number

of different rates allowable must depend on individual demands but for manpower planning where individuals are being scheduled this should not be less than the professional and technical payroll.

6 Calculate staff or basic resource costs separately from transaction costs, and to sort and collate accordingly.

7 Calculate transactions by cost group across activities.

8 Calculate in respect of actual data input, the differences between planned and actual progress on activities, including the value of work done by activity (on the basis of information relating to the percentage completion, against the original budget). Then to aggregate such values, ignoring time delays except where the end date is affected, in which case to bring in the 'penalty cost' and add it to the current costs of those activities causing delay.

9 Carry out normal PERT calculations relating to updating and calculating future schedules.

10 Operate on a multi-project basis, if required, either from one common resource pool or from individual pools for each project.

(iii) Output

1 To print-out as required—by resource, department and project—normal network schedules either in bar chart or listed format by scheduled starts. (As an extension of this facility to draw the control base network, and print relevant data on scheduled starts, planned and actual costs, at the time of review.)

2 To print out cost statements relating to activities, projects and the company similar to those produced by CRD (Computation Research and Development Limited) project costing program. (Some refinements in respect of value of work done would be required if our general suggestions were to be adopted.)

This output should be activity based and should include statements showing planned activity costs, actual cost to date, the debit and credit situation and in addition the value of work done.

A table should then be printed for each project listing all past and present activities and showing planned costs, actuals to date, percentage completions and the values achieved to the

COST ACCOUNTS NOVEMBER 1971

PROJECT NUMBER 990 SUFFIX   ■ — *suffix no. identifies activity*
name of project

PROJECT BEGAN MONTH 10 YEAR 71
PROJECT IS RUN FROM OFFICE ■ OF COMPANY ■
CHARGING PROCEDURE ■

PROJECT DIRECTOR ■   *name of project manager* ■

PERSONNEL COSTS AND CHARGES

MONTH	STAFF NAME	STAFF GRADE	HOURS	DIRECT COSTS	FEE AT ACE RATES *(sales value)*
	names of personnel				
3.	■	■	2.0	■	■
3.	■	■	10.0	■	■
	TOTAL FOR GRADE		12.0		
	TOTAL FOR PERSONNEL COSTS AND CHARGES		12.0	■	■

TRANSACTIONS

MONTH	ITEM	DESCRIPTION		DEBIT	CREDIT
3	1010	V35-3 C R D	JAN	101.100	101.100
3	1010	V40-3 C R D	JAN	212.200	212.200
3	1010	V45-3 C R D	FEB	114.800	114.800
3	1030	GG XEROX CHGS MAR		4.120	4.120
3	1050	GG TRUNK CALLS MA		2.960	2.960
3	1060	V274-3 BURGH FAL		532.080	532.080

coded identification of invoices and vouchers.

TOTAL FOR TRANSACTIONS   967.260   967.260

TOTAL FOR JOB/SUFFIX   ■   ■

ACCUMULATIVE TOTAL AT BEGINNING OF MONTH   ■   ■

ACCUMULATIVE TOTAL AT END OF MONTH   ■   ■

time of update.

This output, illustrated in Fig. 6.4, should then extend to include an aggregate for future planned costs, and the totals of, firstly the 'actuals' to date plus future planned costs, and secondly the estimated activity over-run or under-run.

These should be printed out in both tabular and/or graphical form.

	①	②	③	④	⑤	⑥	⑦	⑧
Activity No.	£ Budget	Cost to date	% complete	£ value	Future planned cost	New projected total cost	Projected saving	Projected loss
100	3,800	1,500	55	2,090	1,710	3,210	590	
110	4,500	3,600	50	2,250	2,250	5,850		1,350
120								
130				etc.				
140								
etc.								
Totals								

Fig. 6.4   Project activity progress summary

  3 To produce separate statements for transactions for each project by cost code, for ledger entry by time period, (the system could well be set up whereby the print-out sheets are the actual ledger sheets) cross-referenced to activity and project.

  4 To produce an invoice summary statement or in a case where there is no outside Client, the cost account for the project manager. (For purposes of invoicing this would suppress actual costs, and deal only in terms of sale value and transactions.)

6.03 The major extensions to currently available software

We have described the basic components of an integrated program combining the features of PERT activity costing and an activity based cost accounting system which ties in directly with the basic accounting records. This may be difficult to achieve but would be extremely useful to any organisation which is project orientated. The major extensions to the present PERT software would be:

1 To exchange the resource-cost scheduling system which averages costs, including overtime, over activities, for a resource cost calculating system which:
   (i)   carries out initial resource levelling;
   (ii) follows (i) with a costing sequence including overtime, where applicable, at different rates. (Not using the 'averaging' technique employed by ICL 1900 Series PERT.)
   (iii) allows the resultant estimates to be examined and amended to meet the budget balancing requirement. (This should be preferably on an interrogative basis—although that is acknowledged to require very substantial computing capacity. CRD have made important advances in the field of time sequencing problems with INTERNET, a software package developed during 1970/1971 for Smiths Industries Ltd.)

2 To allow double entry accounting in the software package. This would widen the scope of input to include debits and credits*. Activity costs and charges would therefore be calculated.

3 To allow overheads to be spread through all relevant activities according to a chosen formula. The proportions of each overhead to be allocated to a range of activities could be specified. (This is a different approach from the hammock activity as it allows direct allocation to specific activities.)

4 To allow for the treatment of transactions in accordance with accounting requirements by incorporating for each transaction an item code (i.e. accounting reference number), in addition to the basic allocation to an activity. This would ensure that for accounts purposes all expenditure on individual items required for financial accounts, for example telephone, travelling, specific materials or

* Facilities included in CRD Limited activity costing software package.

operations and so on would be grouped by activity, project and company, at each update, and printed out as required.

5 To extend the value calculations from the percentage complete of budgeted actual costs, to percentage complete of budgeted charge to date (i.e. sales value), and aggregate such values for comparison by project with actual costs incurred.

6 To extend the range of resource input in order that each member and/or group of a professional team can be scheduled separately.

7 To extend the range of rate calculations to handle individual rates either based on salary/emoluments against a standard hour working year—perhaps with a link back to payroll, or adopting a standard rate per hour or date for each person. This facility should also be adaptable for the costing of operations or of work in progress.

8 To provide the facility to enable all indirect costs to be coded, collated and printed out separately where required, providing the option to either spread overheads on output by activity or to collect them together into one statement. As there may be different appropriate treatment for project overheads and company overheads it should be made possible to apply both options for the same project as required.

9 To provide comprehensive print-outs of activity costs summarised for the project at each review period, listing all used resources and their costs and values. For each activity this would present an assessment of the value to date against the original budget sum and the percentage complete, in terms of both cost and value.

These nine basic requirements which have been listed would in effect produce an income and expenditure account for each project monthly, providing extremely valuable management information. In order to make such a system work the management would have to be prepared to adapt their cost accounting and accounts procedures to an 'activity' or project base. A positive effort would be required to obtain or develop project plans for each main contract, to carry out resource planning and costing, and to ensure that the necessary data collection and analysis procedures were adopted.

6.04 Data requirements

We have described in earlier chapters, the steps which are necessary to organise the administration for this purpose, but it may be useful to look at the data requirements which ensue.

(i) Manpower orientated costing

One of the problems in this field will be to integrate payroll data into the project cost accounting system. It would be desirable to forge a direct link between any existing payroll program and the one proposed. As, however, a separate program may already exist for this specific function, it may be advisable to use basic data relating to salaries, wages, emoluments and other payroll costs to obtain rates per 'standard hour'. This would involve averaging the computations of 'actual' cost into a cost per hour rate, making the resultant calculations slightly incompatible with payroll total.

A compromise between the two approaches would be to use as input the actual payroll cost each month for each person, and divide it by actual hours applicable including holidays and sickness (project overheads). Overheads would then be treated in the normal way and either spread back to current activities or alternatively as specified through the project. Changes in remuneration and consequent rates would be incorporated.

It may be too ambitious to attempt a full cost accounting program using real payroll costs, and from a project control point of view it is certainly as satisfactory to use the average cost per hour approach. Such a system relies heavily on the completion of time sheets by the individuals concerned. The accuracy of these can undoubtedly be improved if the personnel are fully aware of the importance of the data, complete the returns regularly on a short term basis, and if the returns are then carefully checked by the manager concerned.

Overtime creates a difficulty when computing personnel costs and is probably best treated as a transaction, that is as a separate cost. This should be possible with most payroll systems, and it should be input and printed out separately rather than being averaged into an activity rate for that 'resource'. It is in fact a variable cost which should be kept directly under control in relation to the activity budget limits.

In deciding how to deal with the technical programming problems it should be remembered that the important thing is to obtain a sensitivity of project control in the simplest and least onerous way. The emphasis should, therefore, be on obtaining basic data needed for project cost accounting rather than on creating an integrated accounting regime. It is the operational planning and cost accounting which must be integrated rather than the cost accounting and accounting system. Some may disagree with this statement, but may find it costly in computing terms to substantiate their argument. We would, of course, agree that any measure of benefit obtained, for example in the bought ledger, transaction, payroll or invoicing operations, would be highly desirable. It is more important, however, to start by considering the project—cost accounting requirements, and then work back to standard accounting procedures rather than vice versa.

In respect of transactions, the main problems which arise will be to formulate a policy relating to the time base for inclusion in monthly accounts, and also to set down rules for verification and allocation to activities. These problems have also been dealt with at length in other chapters. The time base problem does, however, bear further comment, as it is essential to obtain a statement of project status which is as realistic as possible. The aim should, therefore, be to include in each monthly review all committed costs, that is all those which the organisation has incurred, whether or not an invoice has been received. It cannot be stressed too strongly that the picture obtained, if this simple rule is ignored, can be very misleading.

A further interesting problem which arises in practice is the approach to spreading actual overhead costs which will include management salaries, wage costs for sickness and holidays and so on. There is a strong argument for spreading these pro-rata to the value created, that is in proportion to the amount of the total budgeted sum worked off each month by progress on activities in direct proportion to the value of work done. This seems to be a sensible approach and is relatively simple to apply. Relevant data will be collected in the main from time sheets at project level, coded to one overhead costing number and then spread over current activities in the print out.

(ii) Materials and machine time related costing

So far this book has been basically concerned with manpower costing systems but, where wage and salary costs are a relatively small proportion of the direct costs, it is necessary to adopt methods relevant to the measurement of materials and work in progress. The basic approach should be to develop a network plan for the article which is being assembled or constructed, and then to produce estimates of machine hours and material costs for each activity. A costing sheet similar to that described in Chapter Four should be developed in order to collate these estimates and later to record actual performance.

In practice it should not be more difficult to make these estimates for machine time, assembly and material costs, using standard costing data, once the intellectual problems of producing a representative network have been overcome. The emphasis on activity costs or operational costs rather than on generalised functions within the project may also require some re-thinking in terms of cost estimating procedures.

The main problems which will arise in data estimation and collection revolve around the amount of detail which is demanded by the costing framework. We have already stressed the need to keep this as simple as possible. In this way although costs will be generated by work-piece in terms of machine time, materials and labour, the number of cost centres will be kept within strict limits, leaving more detailed scheduling of intricate sub-operations to subsidiary control procedures or sub-networks.

The systematic completion of job activity sheets will be as vital in the construction or manufacturing processes as that of time sheets is in design or planning projects. Actual costs may, however, be far more difficult to obtain than those for payroll. The project manager will have to rely on standard rates for given operations in work time periods to arrive at resource, operational and activity costs.

In construction and assembly operations, there should be few problems arising from the suggested procedures either in respect of data required, for example relating to machine hours, material and man hours, or in respect of data processing. The scheduling and costing procedures will not differ substantially from those already described. (Different procedures, possibly additional, will be needed to tackle the overall problem of machine loading and sequencing. Machine shop scheduling itself, a far more complex procedure, would be dealt with as a separate procedure providing input to the main cost control system.)

In practice, difficulties may be experienced in estimating the percentage completion of activities at any time when the construction of a building, pipeline or heavy engineering assembly is under review. Methods for measuring such progress will have to be carefully specified, and closely linked in with the collection of data relating to material usage, machine hours and other attributable costs incurred on the shop floor or site. Supervisors will, therefore, have to be carefully trained and instructed in the proposed methods, in the completion of returns and the measurement of work in progress.

If this sounds tedious—and it certainly imposes an administrative load at supervisory level—there is many a famous company whose ex-Chairman must wish he had been able to develop such a costing system.

What we are saying in effect is that standard costing is no more effective than traditional budgetary control methods, unless it is linked directly into operational planning.

Given that the required data relating to actual costs can be collected, it is interesting to examine the double entry idea for computing value which has been described earlier. In the construction or manufacturing fields the idea of 'value added' strikes an interesting chord with accounting principles relating to the valuation of work in progress. A 'conservative' approach would value such work at cost (possibly to include an amount for overheads), in order to compute profit. For project cost control purposes, however, we would suggest that a value added computation related to the overall value of the contract is valid as long as penalty costs are included in the case of delay.

It may be marginally more difficult to evolve an integrated data processing system for operational and financial control in the construction and manufacturing fields, although the basic software would be very similar to that described earlier. The project manager would probably face more complicated problems in data collection and in monitoring progress. However, the most difficult hurdle would be the setting of the correct scale for the project plan in each particular field of operations. This must remain each managements' own decision.

7 A philosophy of management

7.01 General aims of management

There are plenty of theories and systems and schools of management. There are plenty of people who believe in them and plenty of others who do not.

We have met managers who have been so well taught that their every gesture and every action is predictable. These are "systems men", useful executives, but without flair, not good managers. They are generally respected without being admired. They give you the feeling that they are applying their expertise to a project but that they are not living in the project.

On the other hand we have met men who have managed by the sheer weight of their personalities, men whose actions are sometimes illogical, sometimes erratic, but always positive and full-blooded. Such men have the magic of leadership. Other men follow them and work for them as if their lives depended upon it.

We have seen both sorts of men go bankrupt. We have seen both sorts of men succeed. What, then, makes a firm successful?

The first and probably the most important factor is the possession of a good product. All the management techniques put together cannot make a firm successful unless it produces good work which meets the needs of the market.

The second essential factor is the possession of an adequate system of cost control and forward planning. This does not mean that every firm, no matter what it produces, must have a complex system of control; many types of organisation have such regular requirements that only a rudimentary system is needed, but we are convinced that there is a minimum requirement below which no firm can go in a competitive age. We are also convinced that, in any modern enterprise, really good and systematic planning and control can bring nothing but profit.

These, then, are the aims. This book is scarcely concerned with the first but is vitally concerned with the second. We think, however, that the basic necessities for meeting both aims can only be satisfied when management is good and efficient and when staff is good and interested. This book has illustrated a workable system which can be applied with varying degrees of sophistication to different types of project. We have shown how we think these projects should be planned and how their progress should be monitored. We have said little about the managers and the staff.

There are countless books and university courses on the theory of management and we do not propose to launch into a comprehensive review of these. Instead we have thought it appropriate to this book to set down some of the most important aspects of management which have seemed to us, during our business careers, to have been major contributors to success or whose absence have contributed to failure. We have experienced both.

7.02 Organisational structure

We think that it is very important for the morale of individual members of the staff of any organisation that each man knows approximately where he stands in relation to others in the organisation. We have seen the lack of this as being a serious fault in some private organisations; on the other hand we have seen rigid enforcement of a staff structure as being a major drawback to the use of initiative in some large ones. The form of the organisation should be fitted to the type of work it is trying to do and should be sufficiently flexible to allow for a change through time in the objectives of the management of the organisation. Thus, the structure should be as simple as possible and should be such that individuals do not feel themselves being placed in a box in an organisation chart but rather that they are placed at a level in the chart with freedom to move laterally within the level and with access to individuals in the levels immediately above and below their own. Figure 7.1 illustrates

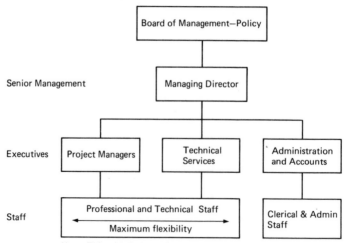

Note: This table is drawn for a typical private firm: similar structures can be drawn for other forms of enterprise, the essential factors being clear chain of command & responsibility and the greatest possible lateral flexibility.

Fig. 7.1 Desirable form of management structure

the type of structure we have in mind.

However, although we want to encourage freedom of movement within the structure, we also think it very important that the main responsibilities of each member of staff are defined in such a way that each man knows what is expected of him, and that such a job specification should be kept continually under review. There is nothing more damaging to morale than to find senior management by-passing people to whom they have given responsibility for an executive function. This practice shows a lack of trust in the executive and should be discouraged vigorously. On the other hand it is good for morale that genuine interest should be shown in the work being done two or three levels down the ladder. It all boils down to the use of common sense and tact.

7.03 Management objectives

When one of the authors first met the other in the course of a review of the workings of the firm, he asked, "what are your objectives in the work you are doing?" The other replied, "to get this b . . . project finished in the next eleven months at the highest possible technical level." This statement started an argument which has led to the present collaboration between us and to the writing of this book and our previous one. We have both realised that there are two sorts of aim, one that of technical excellence and the other that of making a profit. As we said earlier in this chapter you cannot do one without the other and remain solvent and the aim of management is to create conditions in which technical excellence and technical progress can prosper. Hence, Planning for Profit. We showed the range of management purposes in Fig. 1.2 in Chapter One. The more demanding the management purpose, the more elaborate the control structure must be. The essential point is to analyse for each project just what the management purpose is. This should be done well before the start of the project and should be kept in front of the responsible executive throughout its course.

7.04 Labour relations and incentives

We have found that right across the spectrum of our various activities people work best when they feel that they are part of a team with a common purpose, and when they know what that purpose is and what their own efforts are contributing towards achieving it. This was certainly the case in the building of the turbine house frame at Aberthaw described in Chapter Five. The usual method of encouraging people to work hard in the construction industry is to offer them bonus incentives based on productivity. In this case, with its many inter-linked complexities, something better was needed. The procedures were worked out and were explained, with the help of a working model, to all levels of staff involved, and because everyone knew what they had to do and why, labour relations were particularly good.

The same principles produce the same sort of results when applied in offices and factories.

7.05 Technical and administrative clashes

The examples shown in this book are, perhaps, good enough evidence of the need for the understanding of mutual problems between administrators and technical people. We need not dwell on this point except to emphasise that, for a firm to have a successful management control system, both sides of the organisation must be prepared to learn something of the problems and methods of the other. In particular, senior management must appreciate such problems and we have found that the application of the network planning and cost control system advocated in this book can have just this effect.

7.06 Review of techniques

We have been concerned throughout this book mainly with projects involving professional and technical work in offices, but we are sure that the same principles of management can be applied to most other enterprises. Just as a prudent and forward-looking manager of a factory makes periodic reviews of the machinery and tools at his disposal, so should all managers review the routines and techniques they use to control and monitor their work.

They must see whether their current methods of planning and cost control of projects fit properly with their management objectives, and they should introduce techniques like the ones we have described in this book as and when they are needed.

There are very few ideal managers. The mere fact of writing this book has helped each of the authors to identify and correct some of his own shortcomings, and it is our hope that the reader will feel encouraged, as we have been, in his efforts to plan for profit.

Index

Compiled by F.D. Buck

Page references shown in italic
indicate an illustration or a
diagram

117